Barcelona

Dan Colwell

CITYSCAPE

JPMGuides

A quick summary
DISTRICTS AND PRINCIPAL POINTS OF INTEREST

Parc de Pedralbes

Parc Güell

• Estadi del F.C. Barcelona (Camp Nou)

Eixample & Gràcia

• Pl. de Sants

Sagrada Família •

La Pedrera •

Pl. de Catalunya •

MACBA •

• Poble Espanyol

El Raval

Catedral La Seu •

Palau Güell •

Ciutat Vella

Plaça Reial •

Rambles

Museu Picasso •

Montjuïc

• Museu Nacional d'Art de Catalunya (MNAC)

Parc de la Ciutadella

Parc de Montjuïc

Castell •

Aquàrium de Barcelona •

Hafen

• La Barceloneta

The historic centre of Barcelona is the Ciutat Vella (Old Town), the site of the original Roman settlement and later the basis of the Barri Gòtic, or medieval quarter. The rest of the city is easily reached from here, either on foot or by public transport.

Some figures

1,6 million inhabitants
2,000 years of history
9 UNESCO-listed sites
7,4 million visitors p.a.
4 km of sandy beaches
11 metro lines
1,100 ha of public green spaces
55 museums
2,000 Modernista buildings

Contents

Symbols

- ★ Our favourites
- ✪ Metro
- ▰ RENFE
- ▰ FGC

cityLights

Within minutes of your very first walk along La Rambla you'll realise that you're in one of the most exciting cities in the world. This long street running through the old town simply fizzes with energy. And yet far from being an exception, La Rambla sets the tone for all of Barcelona. The city has plenty to be excited about. Its dynamism and diversity extend from an ebullient café culture and exuberant nightlife to ultra-modern centres of contemporary art and cutting-edge urban developments.

There are world-class museums devoted to Picasso and Miró, and in the Barri Gòtic the city has the most well-preserved medieval quarter in Europe. It is also home to the extraordinary architecture of Antoni Gaudí, the presiding genius of Modernisme, the home-grown version of Art Nouveau.

Barceloneses can ruminate on all this at any number of restaurants, where they will be served first-rate Catalonian cuisine with its own deliciously earthy and proud tradition separate from the rest of Spain.

◀ *Gaudí's "La Pedrera" is one of the most outstanding buildings of the 20th century.*

Like much else in Barcelona, lunch and dinner are occasions which start later and continue longer than in many other major business cities. And when they want to get away from the bustle of the city, they could be lying on a beach, skiing in the mountains or sampling wines at vineyards in rolling countryside all within a few hours of the centre.

Canny Catalonians

This vibrant metropolis of just over 1,6 million people has long enjoyed a reputation in Spain for its business acumen and industriousness, and the citizens pride themselves on their *seny*, the Catalan word for a solid, commonsense approach to life. For centuries Barcelona has been the economic powerhouse of the country. It's the birthplace of Spain's industrial revolution, the foremost port in the Mediterranean, and the commercial focus of the country's connection to the rest of Europe. But it's not just because of this that Barceloneses look away from Madrid and see themselves as more like their northern counterparts in Paris or London. For apart from being undoubtedly cosmopolitan, they also think of their city as a national capital and never miss an opportunity to express their desire for independence; and the push for total autonomy from Spain is as strong as ever.

Until the end of the 15th century, Barcelona was at the centre of an independent Catalan state, which had its own laws and language, and even ran a Mediterranean empire. Although the empire was lost, its collective *seny* remained intact and the city continued to prosper. Thankfully, though, Catalonian common sense sometimes goes magnificently awry, and it is the moments of wild extravagance that we can thank for such extraordinary monuments as the fairytale Parc Güell, the surreal Magic Fountain near Plaça Espanya, and the city waterfront, renovated for the 1992 Olympic Games.

Maybe it's their innate democratic spirit, or maybe it's because they identify with a proud, independent creature intimidated by superior Castilian firepower, but the fact is that the Catalans have never really taken to bullfighting. Until a few years ago there were two bullrings in Barcelona, but then the Catalan government flexed its muscles. Tens of thousands of anti-bullfight signatures were collected, and in late 2011, bullfighting was banned altogether. With typical Catalan Fair, one ring—Las Arenas—has been converted into a stunning shopping and entertainment complex (see p. 64) whilst talks are in progress with a view to making La Monumental, on the opposite side of the city side, into a giant mosque.

See it from on high

The people's love affair with their city is all too evident. Over the centuries they have created an abundance of viewpoints from which to admire it. Try the Columbus Monument for a superb vista of the revamped old port. Or in the centre of the Gothic Quarter, find your way up to the roof of the cathedral, from where Barcelona's medieval world of high-altitude gargoyles, terracotta rooftops and hidden courtyards is magically revealed. The 19th-century expansion of the city, the Eixample, provides a remarkable highpoint —the other-worldly spire of the Sagrada Família church is guaranteed to give you an unforgettable perspective on Barcelona. The lucky Barceloneses have, of course, been helped along by Mother Nature, who did her bit by providing some perfectly placed hills around the edge of town. Since 1992, the loftiest panorama has been from the Collserola tower on top of Mount Tibidabo. Here, the whole of Barcelona is laid out spectacularly before you.

istockphoto.com/Martinez Banus

cityPast

Legend has it that Barcelona was founded by the Carthaginians, who had settlements along Spain's Mediterranean coast, and that it was named after their leader Hamil Barca, father of Hannibal. In fact, the earliest-known settlers in the region were the Laietani, a Bronze Age Celt-Iberian tribe who specialized in producing grain and harvesting oysters, and there was no town established here until the Romans turned up some time in the 1st century BC. Their main centre was at Tarragona, to the south, and at first Barcelona was just a military camp. It became an official colony around 15 BC under the Emperor Augustus, and was given the name Faventia Julia Augusta Pia Barcino.

◀ *During your sightseeing you will come across charming historic houses and elaborately decorated façades.*

istockphoto.com/Amorim

The town remained a minor, albeit prosperous outpost for 200 years, known mainly for its manufacture of wine, olive oil and garum, a fermented anchovy sauce that was exported throughout the empire. It had a Jewish community in place by the 2nd century, and around the year 300 acquired its first patron saint, the Christian martyr Santa Eulàlia. But the secure life of a Mediterranean colony was under threat. The empire was facing invasion from northern barbarians and the city walls had to be strengthened with huge stone blocks during the 4th century, many of which are still visible today.

Of Visigoths, Moors and Franks

From 409, successive waves of Vandal, Alani and Suevian tribes swept over the Pyrenees and invaded Spain. Each one ransacked Barcelona and then headed south, so when the Visigoths entered the city in 415 under King Ataulf and made it the centre of their new kingdom, the inhabitants were at least promised some stability. Indeed, the Visigoth occupation was to last three centuries and eventually extended to almost the whole of Spain. The new rulers turned out to be great believers in jurisprudence, embellishers of churches and altogether most un-barbarian in character. A series of baronies evolved under the central authority of the king, but by the 8th century the system was disintegrating, with the king and his barons in perpetual conflict.

Such political disunity was an open invitation to the next invader eyeing up Spain's rich lands, though this time the danger lay to the south. In 711, Arab armies crossed the Straits of Gibraltar from Africa and overwhelmed the Visigoths. They reached Barcelona six years later and continued on into southern France, where they stayed until defeated by the Franks under Charlemagne at the end of the 8th century. The Franks pushed the Moors back across the Pyrenees, and in 801 Barcelona was liberated by Charlemagne's son, Louis the Pious. It then became part of Louis's Marca Hispánica (Spanish March), a buffer zone between Moorish Spain and the Frankish empire that occupies roughly the area of modern Catalonia. Given that the Moors would stay in Spain for nearly seven more centuries, Catalonia's cultural and linguistic separateness from the rest of the country, and its fierce sense of independence, can be dated from this time.

The Franks left the region under the command of a number of counts, who guarded the border and fought off Moorish incursions. One of them was the Count of Barcelona, Guifré el Pilós (Wilfred the Hairy), a man famous not just for the abundance of his body hair, but also for establishing something approaching a Catalonian state towards the end of the 9th century. He did it by conquering the various counties of the Spanish March and uniting them under his rule, which afterwards became hereditary. Catalonia was still nominally in the Frankish domain. But when the Moors raided Barcelona in 985, and the request for aid from the Franks was ignored, Wilfred's great-grandson, Borrell II, used the occasion to declare Catalonian independence.

Medieval Golden Age

Barcelona entered the new millennium in upbeat mood. Either by marriage or purchase, successive counts had set about acquiring more territory. The city's economy was starting to boom, and a code of law known as the Usatges, an early sort of Magna Carta, had been instituted by Ramon Berenguer I in 1064–68 guaranteeing the rights of citizens. Things were shaping up nicely for a Catalan Golden Age.

It began in earnest in 1137, when Count Ramon Berenguer IV married Petronella, the heiress to the throne of Catalonia's neighbouring state of Aragon, and received the

Santa Eulàlia is the heart of the Old Town.

Huber/Ripani

Ingrid Morató

whole kingdom as a dowry. With the new title of Count-King *(comte-rei)*, and a greatly increased military and financial capability, Barcelona's rulers began to harbour dreams of empire, and looked out to the Mediterranean as the place where they would be realised.

Under Jaume I (1213–76) and his immediate descendants through to the middle of the 14th century, Catalonia conquered the Balearic Islands, Sardinia, Sicily and established trading posts as far as Athens, Constantinople and Beirut. Catalonian merchants flourished, and the wealth they created flowed back into the city, funding the construction of Barcelona's Barri Gòtic, with its magnificent Gothic cathedral, churches and mansions. Meanwhile, Catalan became established as a literary language, with translations of the Bible and the Classics, Jaume I's autobiographical *Book of Deeds* about his military exploits, and other works of philosophy and poetry being written in it.

Catalonia Falls, Spain Rises

Even as Barcelona reached its peak of achievement in the reign of Pere III (1336–87), when the Saló del Tinell, the Drassanes shipyard and much of the cathedral were built, things were already beginning to fall apart. In 1348 the city was devastated by the Black Death, which reached it via the colony of Mallorca. In the wake of the plague came famine and epidemics, and in 1391 a terrible pogrom was carried out against the Jews, who were blamed for the disasters.

The unbroken line of Counts of Barcelona stretching back to Wilfred the Hairy ended with

◀ *Christopher Columbus points out the way.*

the death of Martí I in 1410, and the throne passed to Ferdinand of Antequera. From now on, Catalonia would be ruled by Castilians. As the 15th century progressed, the great days of Catalan power slowly trickled away. Mercantile rivals such as the Genoese and the Venetians began to dominate Mediterranean trade. In 1462 a 10-year civil war broke out between the monarchy and the Catalan upper classes. Soon after it had ended, the new king, Ferdinand II, married the future Isabella I of Castile, and Spain was united as a single nation.

The main effect was to shift political power from Barcelona to Madrid, something that was compounded by Christopher Columbus's discovery of the Americas in 1492, after which Spain's gaze was fixed firmly westwards away from the Mediterranean. Worse still, Catalans were barred from trading with the New World colonies. Madrid became the official capital of the empire in 1561 under the Habsburg king of Spain, Philip II, while Catalonia suffered the indignity of having a Habsburg viceroy imposed upon it.

Disaffection mounted, and in 1640 a popular uprising by peasants (known as the War of the Reapers) saw Catalonia declare its independence from Spain. Twelve years of war left the region exhausted and back under the control of Madrid. Then, during the War of Spanish Succession that followed the end of the Habsburg line in 1700, Catalonia sided with the English, Dutch

Trace Catalonia's past in the Museu d'Història de Catalunya. ▶

Jaume Meneses

and Germans against the Bourbon candidate, Philip V. When their allies signed the Treaty of Utrecht leaving Philip V on the throne, the Catalans had to face the consequences, and Barcelona was besieged by Spanish troops once again. This time, a huge fort, the Ciutadella, was built to keep an eye on the unruly Catalans, their ancient city government was dismantled, and the use of the Catalan language in writing and education was banned.

The Catalan Renaissance

Oddly enough, one result of Catalonia's fuller absorption into the Spanish state was a turnaround in its economic position. This was mainly due to the development of the cotton industry and, from 1778, the lifting of the ban on trade with the Americas. There was a temporary setback when Barcelona was caught up in the turmoil of the Napoleonic Wars and occupied by French troops, but by the middle of the 19th century the city had regained its confidence, which had risen to a level not seen since the Middle Ages.

Like then, this was manifested in two important fields, architecture and the Catalan language. New works of literature in Catalan were published and the Institute of Catalan Studies was set up in 1906. But Barcelona's cultural dynamism was most evident in the remarkable buildings that went up at the end of the 19th century. The huge extension of the city beyond the old town—the Eixample—began in 1860, and over the following decades its great boulevards became home to some of Barcelona's most radical Modernista (Art Nouveu) architecture, commissioned by the wealthy middle classes and designed by leading Catalan architects such as Antoni Gaudí and Lluís Domènech i Montaner. The focal point of this Renaixença (Renaissance), as the period came to be called, was the Universal Exposition of 1888. It proved to be a dazzling showcase for Barcelona's industrial and cultural talent, and attracted one and a half million visitors—and yet, with the splendid array of new building projects it engendered, it almost bankrupted the city.

◀ *Demonstration during the Tragic Week of 1909.*

Civil War and General Franco

Alongside the prosperity, however, there grew a dissatisfied class of poor workers. Anarchist and republican groups developed with the aim of challenging the established order, and with an influx of immigrants from other parts of Spain adding to the mix, the early 20th century saw increasing social and political upheaval. This culminated in the Setmana Tràgica, or Tragic Week in 1909, when workers rioted against conscription for a colonial war in Morocco and set fire to churches. In retaliation, they were shot down by troops, and later their leaders were rounded up and five of them executed.

A strong Catalan separatist movement developed around this time as well, and on the back of its industrial success the region was able to regain some of the political autonomy lost in the 18th century. With Spain a non-combatant, Barcelona did well out of World War I by supplying arms and equipment to the French. Its continuing role as the nation's economic powerhouse was demonstrated once more in the 1929 International Exhibition, in preparation for which the Montjuïc and Plaça d'Espanya areas were given extensive overhauls.

Things turned dramatically for the worse in the 1930s, however, when Spain's newly elected Republican government was overthrown by right-wing forces under General Franco. The city lived up to its longstanding radical tradition and proved the main centre of resistance against Franco, but was defeated in January 1939. As with Philip V two centuries earlier, reprisals took the form of withdrawal of Catalan political and linguistic rights. The city now entered its grey period, with 20 years of economic and cultural repression.

Barcelona Today

Barcelona was bouncing back even before the death of General Franco in 1975, benefiting financially from the new industry of mass tourism on the nearby Costa Brava. Within two years of the end of Franco's rule, democratic elections were held and Catalonia regained its regional political authority, the Generalitat, under a Catalan president, Jordi Pujol. Barcelona soon re-established itself as the most fast-paced, industrious and above all stylish city in Spain. Education, literature and even the street signs were now in Catalan.

In 1992 Barcelona used the occasion of the Olympics to transform itself. In particular, the old, disused waterfront on the northern swathe received a facelift and gave the city a fine new leisure area which has now been joined by a high tech business district known as 22@.

In 2008 the global economic meltdown —*El Crisis*—slowed down the city's relentless pace of construction and expansion. Although unemployment in Catalonia is high, and austerity measures have made a tangible impact on many of its inhabitants, the region has fared well compared to many of its southern counterparts, and tourism remains strong.

Torre Porta Fira on Plaça ▶
d'Europa, by Toyo Ito.

citySights

◀ *La Rambla, the busiest and most colourful*
   pedestrian mall in Barcelona

LA RAMBLA

Enthralling and dramatic, La Rambla is one of the world's most spectacular shows, the cast made up of the thousands of people who continually pass up and down along the swirling patterns of its blue and grey paving stones. To add to the fun, it's packed with newsstands, street performers, ice-cream stalls and, despite a recent crack-down on the La Rambla's steamier side, three-card tricksters and small-time hustlers. In fact, this glorious 2-kilometre, tree-lined boulevard has so much for the eye to take in that it can feel ten times as long, and yet still you can't help but agree with the Spanish poet García Lorca when he said that he wished it would never end.

THE DISTRICT AT A GLANCE

La Rambla (map 2, W2–Y7) It first took on its modern appearance in the 18th century, and the slightly meandering shape of the street is due to the fact that it was laid over a dry riverbed along whose banks the western wall of the medieval Barri Gòtic had been built (the name comes from the Arabic word *ramla*, meaning "riverbed"). It runs from the vast Plaça de Catalunya down to the Columbus statue and the port, and strictly speaking changes its name five times along the way, with each part of the boulevard recording the names of convents or churches it once passed. Look at the street signs as you go and you'll see you're actually on Rambla de Canaletes, dels Estudis, de Sant Josep, dels Caputxins and de Santa Monica. It's best to simply join the stream of people and enjoy the unrivalled pleasure of the *paseo* here. But a few notable sights

All the colour and life of Spain concentrated in postcards on the Rambla.

en route are worth pausing over—and don't forget to look at the fascinating upper storeys of the buildings. ❖ Catalunya, Liceu, Drassanes

Mercat de la Boqueria (map 2, W4) Barcelona's most important food market was built in the 19th century. Beneath its vast network of wrought-iron vaulting is a truly mouth-watering display of fruit and nuts, spices and herbs, and mounds of fish, sausages, meat and cheeses, takeaway fruit and juices. • Mon–Sat 8am–8.30pm ☎ 93 318 25 84 • La Rambla 91 ❖ Liceu

Museu de l'Eròtica (map 2, X4) On the other side of La Rambla from the market, this attempt to give a serious historical perspective on the subject of all things erotic is not entirely convincing. But some of its displays, such as the collection of photos depicting Barcelona's racy Barri Xino district in the 1930s, are fascinating. • Daily 10 am–midnight ☎ 93 318 98 65 • La Rambla 96 ❖ Liceu

Plaça Reial (map 2, X5) Just off La Rambla, and reached by the narrow C/de Colom, the Plaça Reial is an impressive 19th-century square of handsome neo-classical façades. The two lampposts in the centre are the earliest known work of the great Modernista architect, Antoni Gaudí. The palm-shaded square, built on the site of a Capuchin convent, attracts an odd social mix, which it just about manages to balance harmoniously: its colonnades harbour several bars and a couple of trendy restaurants, yet for some time it has also had a well-earned reputation for being the hangout of the city's down-and-outs. For a less edgy experience, visit it during the day. ◆ Liceu

THE ART OF STANDING STILL

There was a time when it seemed that La Rambla attracted as many mime artists as tourists. But though some of them aspired to follow in the noble tradition of Marcel Marceau, an increasing number appeared to have sought an income simply by spraying themselves in silver paint and standing still for a few hours. This wasn't good enough for the exacting aesthetic demands of the Ajuntament, which clearly felt that these human statues were letting down the reputation of the famous street. Thus in 2007 new rules were brought in restricting the number of performers on La Rambla and creating authorized spots where they could stand. Furthermore, they would only be allowed to use homemade costumes and were banned from using masks, animals as props and forcing the public to pay for photos. A window of opportunity was kept open for other artists such as magicians, dancers and Joan Sabaté, known as the Maradona de La Rambla and master of the art of "keepy-uppy". They can perform on the Rambla de Santa Mónica, or the southern stretch towards the Monument a Colom, judged to be the less prestigious end—artistically speaking, that is—of La Rambla.

hemis/Rieger

Halfway down La Rambla at Plaça de la Boqueria, the mosaic is by Joan Miró.

Museu de Cera (map 2, Y6) A small passage leads to the Wax Museum, in the grand neoclassical premises of a former credit bank. Children love the tableaux, chamber of horrors, and models of well-known figures such as General Franco and Princess Diana. Next door, the Passatge del Temps (Time Tunnel) has a fascinating collection of curios, whilst the Bosc de les Fades Café is replete with fairytale installations • July–Sept daily 10am–10pm; Oct–June Mon–Fri 10am–1.30pm, 4–7.30pm; Sat, Sun 11am–2pm, 4.30–8.30pm ☎ 93 317 26 49 • Passatge de la Banca 7 ✣ Drassanes

Monument a Colom (map 2, Y7) This tall column was built for the Universal Exposition of 1888 and is Barcelona's homage to Christopher Columbus. His discovery of America spelt the end of Catalonia's economic independence from Castile, but Columbus has remained a hero in Barcelona. A small lift inside the column takes visitors to the mirador for excellent views. • Daily 8.30am–8.30pm (7.30 pm in winter) • Plaça Portal de la Pau ✣ Drassanes

WALKING TOUR: LA RAMBLA

The **Font de Canaletes** is just south of Plaça de Catalunya, a drinking fountain from which a taste of the water is said to guarantee a return trip to Barcelona. On the left-hand side of La Rambla here is the **Hotel Continental**, where George Orwell stayed with his wife during the Spanish Civil War and, curiously, went back to for dinner while on active duty at the **Teatre Poliorama**, further down on the right. He spent a few days on the roof there, training his rifle on the Civil Guards holed up at the old **Cafè Moka** opposite (now a restaurant), complaining more of boredom than of fear. These days the theatre is a place where visitors will be enlivened by performances of classical music, jazz and flamenco. A short way along is the **Església de Betlem**. Don't expect the interior to match the baroque splendour of the façade—it was burned by Republicans in 1936. Just beyond this is the start of what's known as the **Rambla de les Flors**, home to the flower stalls that make this one of the most photographed parts of the avenue. On the right, close to the landmark **Mercat de la Boqueria**, be sure to take in the fine neoclassical exterior of the **Palau de la Virreina** at La Rambla 99. The name means Palace of the Viceroy's Wife, and it was built in the 1770s by a returning viceroy of Peru. It now functions as a cultural centre with temporary exhibitions. The Boqueria market caters to just about every dietary craving, but in one thing at least is outdone by **Escribà**, at La Rambla 83. This family-run confectioners, with a classic Modernista mosaic shop front, sells spectacularly inventive chocolates and pastries and is a magnet for people from across Barcelona who are in need of a little self-indulgence. Across from Escribà, look where you're treading—there's a large **pavement mosaic** designed in typically bold primary colours by Joan Miró in 1976. On the left, where the roads converge from the Barri Gòtic, the extraordinary **Casa Bruno Cuadros** (1883) is decorated with umbrellas (it was once an umbrella factory) and has an intriguing green Chinese dragon acting as a lamp holder. There's no better place to round off this walking tour than at La Rambla's best café, the grand fin de siècle **Cafè de l'Òpera**, a few steps south from the Casa Bruno Cuadros. Named for the **Gran Teatre del Liceu** opposite, it's great for such treats as tapas, *xurros amb xocolata* (fried dough and chocolate), and for relaxed people-watching.

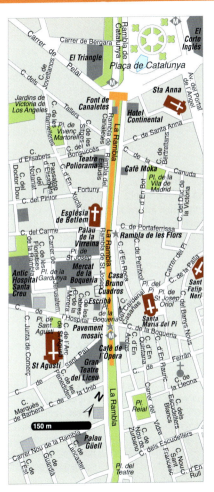

The city's most famous thoroughfare from north to south

Start:
Font de Canaletes
✧ Catalunya

Finish:
Cafè de l'Òpera
✧ Liceu

ART IN CATALONIA

Catalonia has a long history as one of the world's great centres of art, going back to the Pyrenean church frescoes of the 12th century and the Golden Age of 15th-century Catalan Gothic painting by artists like Bernat Martorell and Jaume Huguet. However, with the opening up of the New World, political and economic power drained away from Barcelona towards Madrid, and Catalonian independence withered. Along with it went the country's artistic supremacy, until the resurgence of Catalonia in the 19th century. Its main cultural expression at that time was in the architectural glory of Modernisme; but Catalonia's artistic reputation was to be restored in the 20th century by that great triumvirate of avant-garde painters, Pablo Picasso, Joan Miró and Salvador Dalí.

Pablo Picasso (1881–1973)

Picasso's connection with Barcelona started when his father moved there from Malaga in 1895 to teach at La Llotja art academy, at which the 13-year-old Pablo enrolled as a student. He stayed in Catalonia for just nine years before leaving for Paris, but in that time had developed from a child prodigy into a fully fledged artist. It was in Barcelona that he received his first ever paid commission—designing the menu cover for Els Quatre Gats, the café in the Barri Gòtic where he and his circle of radical artists liked to hang out—and also where he created the major works of his Blue Period.

But above all, Barcelona is where Picasso found the initial inspiration to make the first rupture with traditional Western art forms. Looking at the remarkable series of works on display in the Museu Picasso in the Born district, one can sense the influence of the elongated Catalan Gothic sculptures and also of the Catalonian art of *trencadis*—the use of broken pieces of ceramic beloved of Modernista architects. No history of Cubism and fragmentation in modern art could be complete without considering the impact of Gaudí on Picasso, who lived for a while on the Carrer Nou de la Rambla and passed the Palau Güell almost every day. One might argue by dramatically affecting Picasso, Barcelona had a profound influence on 20th century art as a whole.

Marco Papale

Museu
Picasso

Joan Miró (1893–1983)

Joan Miró was the son of a watchmaker. After working for two years as an office clerk and suffering a nervous breakdown as a consequence, he was allowed by his parents to study at an art college in Barcelona. His teacher introduced him to contemporary French art and, significantly, medieval Catalan church frescoes and the buildings of Gaudí. Miró was especially captivated by the serpentine benches of the Parc Güell. From an early stage his paintings and sculptures tended towards Surrealism and Dadaism, and he took part in the First Surrealist Exhibition in Paris in 1925. With its emphasis on content and free form, Surrealism was the means by which Miró explored personal fantasies, both conscious and unconscious. But despite the apparently abstract nature of his work, the artist insisted that, "for me a form is never something abstract; it is always a sign of something… a man, a bird, or something else." One of the most fascinating elements of any visit to the Fundació Joan Miró on Montjuïc is encountering Miró's "signs" and pondering on their meanings.

Salvador Dalí (1904–89)

The paintings of the most outrageous—and best known—of the Surrealists follow a different route to the unconscious than those of Miró. Deeply influenced by Freud, they forego Miró's signs for meticulously detailed and recognizable images from the real world that are placed in bizarre or irrational situations, often in brightly sunlit landscapes that recall Dalí's Catalonian homeland around Figueres, north of Barcelona. This strange dreamlike world of melting watch faces and spindly legged elephants is, of course, Dalí's way of evoking what he called the "greater reality" of the subconscious mind, with its uncontrollable and erotic energy. His career at the forefront of Surrealism lasted little more than a decade. By the late 1930s, Dalí, always an artist of profound technical ability, had moved to a more academic style and was expelled from the Surrealist movement. There's no better place to confront the artist at his most surreal than the Dalí-designed Teatre-Museu Dalí in Figueres.

CIUTAT VELLA

Facing the sea, the historic old town lies to the left of La Rambla. The first Roman settlers had their main temple and forum on what is now Plaça Sant Jaume, which has remained the centre of civic life in Catalonia to this day. Most of the architectural treasures of the Barri Gòtic (Gothic Quarter) date from the medieval era, however, and include the magnificent cathedral, royal palace and an atmospheric tangle of narrow streets. Beyond here is the pretty Ciutadella park, with a couple of fine museums, and Barcelona's No. 1 crowd-puller, the Museu Picasso.

THE DISTRICT AT A GLANCE

Basílica de Santa Maria del Pi (map 2, X4) If you enter the Ciutat Vella from La Rambla at Plaça Boqueria, you will soon arrive at this classic example of Catalan Gothic architecture. It was begun in 1319, though the octagonal bell tower was added in the following century. The dark, almost austere interior, with its

Each of the thirteen geese in the cathedral cloister represents one year in the life of Santa Eulàlia, a 4th-century martyr.

superb single-span nave, is typically Catalan, and the splendid rose window over the entrance is by far the most flamboyant gesture. On the first and third Friday, Saturday and Sunday of every month the area is taken over by an artisan food market and every weekend there is a good outdoor art market. • Mon–Sat 10am–7pm (6pm in winter), Sun 4–8pm (7pm in winter) ☎ 93 318 47 43 • Plaça del Pi ✿ Liceu

Caelum (map 2, X4) Over 30 monastery kitchens and convents supply food to this restaurant-shop behind the Palau Episcopal: olives, cheeses, chocolates etc. Food is served in the basement, in a former Jewish bath house. • Mon–Thurs 10.30am–8.30pm, Fri, Sat 10.30am–11pm, Sun 10.30am–9pm ☎ 93 302 69 93 • C/de la Palla 8 ✿ Liceu

Catedral de Santa Eulàlia (map 2, Y3) Barcelona's spectacular Gothic cathedral is built on a site first occupied by a Roman temple, and later a mosque. The earliest parts of the cathedral date from 1298, and work continued through to the 1440s—though a shortage of cash meant that the façade had to wait until 1890 to be completed, in what some purists consider an overly ornate Gothic Revival style. Inside, elegant, slender pillars soar upwards, marking off the nave from its two aisles, which boast an array of 29 side chapels. The centre of the cathedral is dominated by the *coro*, a characteristi-

LA SARDANA

The energetic yet graceful national dance of Catalonia, the *sardana*, with its haunting woodwind accompaniment, hypnotizes Catalans wherever they may be. The deceptively simple-looking *sardana* is danced in normal everyday clothes, except on special occasions. The dancers form a circle, which grows as newcomers join it. If it proves unwieldy, they just form another. If they run out of space, they make circles within circles. Each group has a leader who keeps meticulous time and signals changes. If he makes one error his ring loses its rhythm and can't complete the final step in time with the band. The wonder of the *sardana* is the spirit it generates. Doctors and farmers dance together; long-haired students join the same circle as middle-aged housewives. Even tourists can, technically, join in, though a fairly strict rule puts an end to most outsiders' ambitions: no Catalan would ever move into a circle that has standard of dancing too high for him, and uninitiated visitors might thus find themselves edged out.

In Barcelona, the *sardana* is danced in front of the cathedral Saturdays at 6pm and Sundays at 11.15.

Florence Segura

cally Spanish feature where the carved choir stalls are enclosed within a box-like structure. Between this and the altar, steps lead down to the crypt containing the tomb of Barcelona's patron saint, Eulàlia. Possibly the most beautiful part of the cathedral is the medieval cloister. Among the Gothic arches, ancient tombstones and tall palm trees, you'll find a gaggle of geese. This eccentric touch goes back centuries—one explanation is that the whiteness of their plumage was intended to evoke the purity of Saint Eulàlia. The Chapter House has a small museum of art, with paintings by Renaissance Catalan artists such as Jaume Huguet and Bartolomé Bermejo. The cloister gives access to the Romanesque Capella de Santa Llúcia, predating the rest of the cathedral.

• Cathedral: Mon–Sat 8am–13.45pm, 5.15–7.30pm, Sun and holidays 8am–13.45pm, 5.15–7.30pm. Entrance is free but the cloister, museum and roof carry an entry fee). VIP visits Mon–Sat 1–5pm, Sun 2–5pm (paid entrance with less crowds and includes after-hours entrance to the museum. During mass, access to the cathedral is limited) ☎ 93 342 82 62 • Plaça de la Seu 3 ✢ Liceu, Jaume I

Casa de l'Ardiaca (map 2, X3) Leaving the Santa Llúcia chapel by its door onto the street outside, you will find yourself opposite the former archdeacon's house. Dating from the 16th century, it has an exquisite cloister-courtyard with a small fountain and 100-year-old palm tree. The building now holds the city's historic archives, but the general public are welcome inside (ID is required).
• Sep–June: Mon–Fri 9am–8.45pm, Sat 9am–1pm. July–Aug: Mon–Fri 9am–7.30pm ☎ 93 318 11 95 • C/de Santa Llúcia 1 ✢ Liceu, Jaume I

Museu Diocesà (map 2, Y3) Head back to Plaça de la Seu, where this museum is located in the Casa de la Pia Almoina, a 15th-century almshouse that incorporates part of a Roman tower. The works on display represent mainly religious art dating from the Gothic era, including paintings, sculptures and altarpieces. • Tues–Fri 11am–6pm, Sat 11am–2pm and 2.30pm to 6pm, Sun 11am–2pm ☎ 93 315 22 13 • Av. de la Catedral 4 ✢ Jaume I

Museu Frederic Marès (map 2, Y3) Follow the narrow C/dels Comtes to one of Barcelona's more unusual museums. Frederic Marès (1893–1991) was a sculptor, art teacher and obsessive collector of anything and everything that came his way. The display truly ranges from the sublime to the ridiculous—a vast quantity of religious sculptures, especially crucifixions and statues of the Virgin, alongside displays of such fripperies as ashtrays, cigarette cards, nut-crackers and perfume flasks. This vast store of objects was given by Marès to the city, and is now housed in a wing of the Palau Reial. • Tues–Sat 10am–7pm, Sun 11am–8pm ☎ 93 256 35 00 • Plaça Sant Iu 5–6 ◈ Jaume I

MUHBA – Museu d'Història de Barcelona (map 2, Y3–4) Turn left off C/dels Comtes to the well-preserved medieval Plaça del Rei, once the courtyard of the **Palau Reial Major**, the grand royal palace of the Count-Kings of Barcelona. Most of the grand edifices laid out before you can be seen inside on a ticket to the MUHBA, as well as more ancient relics from the city's Roman origins (see p. 33) and a portrait gallery of famous Catalans and other histori-cal paintings. In the north corner of the square, steps lead up to the magnifi-cent 14th-century **Saló del Tinell**, with its remarkable barrel-like vault and arch-es that span 17 m. Historians are undecided as to whether it was in here or on the steps outside that Ferdinand and Isabella received Columbus after his return from the Americas. The hall was later used by the Spanish Inquisition as an imposing place of interrogation.

The adjacent **Capella de Santa Àgata** was built under Jaume II at the begin-ning of the 14th century as the palace chapel. The 5-storey **Mirador del Rei Martí** (King Martin's watchtower) that overlooks the Plaça del Rei is a later addition (16th century).

The MUHBA is entered via the **Casa Padellàs**, a 15th-century mansion that was moved here from nearby C/de Mercaders in 1931. During the work, the foundations of a substantial part of the original Roman city were discovered, and these now form the most fascinating part of the museum. Descend by lift to a series of boardwalks that extend beneath Plaça del Rei as far as the cathe-dral. These take you over ancient roads, houses, shops and factories for making wine, salted fish and garum, a fish sauce highly regarded by the Romans. Upstairs, you'll find exhibitions on the history of the city, from sacred objects to the bomb thrown into patrons at the Liceu Opera House in 1893, and access to the interiors of the Palau Reial. • Tues–Sat 10am–7pm, Sun 10am–8pm. Ticket allows access to various other sites, including the Monestir de Pedral-bles (p. 81) ☎ 93 256 21 00 • Plaça del Rei ◈ Jaume I

Palau de la Generalitat (map 2, Y4) Plaça St Jaume is the epicentre of Barcelona's political life. The Generalitat—the Catalan regional government—has been on the north side of the square since the 15th century. The façade is a late-Renaissance addition—but the original Gothic entrance, with a fine sculpture of St George dating from 1418, is by master Catalan architect Marc Safont. It can be seen on C/del Bisbe around the corner. Access to the building is limited. If you are able to get in, though, you'll find a beautiful medieval cloister and Safont's magnificent chapel of Sant Jordi (St George, Catalonia's patron saint). • **Open for guided tours on the 2nd and 4th Sun of each month, 10.30am–1.30pm. Booking required through website: www.gencat.cat** • Pl. Sant Jaume ✧ Jaume I

THE TRAGIC CALL

West of Plaça Sant Jaume is the Call, the former Jewish area of Barcelona. The first Jews settled here in the 2nd century, long before there were any Christians here. By the Middle Ages they were the backbone of the flourishing financial and mercantile community and under-pinned the burgeoning Mediterranean empire of the Count-Kings. That didn't prevent their victimization by the authorities. Jews had to pay heavy taxes, while they had to spend the hours of darkness inside the Call. During the 13th century, under Jaume I, they were forced to wear a red and yellow button on their clothes so they could be easily identified. Worse was to follow. Blamed by the populace for the recent plague, a terrible pogrom was carried out in August 1391 and the community massacred. By the time Jews were officially banned from the city in 1424, the Call was already deserted. Walk the tiny side streets of the district around Carrer del Call and Carrer de Ramon del Call and you could fancy yourself back in medieval Barcelona—except that the traces of the community which gave so much to the city have virtually disappeared. To find out more, visit the remains of the medieval **Synagogue** (C/Marlet 5, ☎ 93 317 07 90, Summer: Mon–Fri 10.30am–6.30pm, Sat–Sun 10.30am– 2.30pm; Winter: Mon–Fri 11am–5.30pm, Sat–Sun 11am–3pm), or the **MUHBA El Call** (Placeta de Manuel Ribé, ☎ 93 256 21 22, Tue–Fri 11am–2pm, Sat–Sun 11am–7pm) where you will find information and exhibitions.

Temple d'August (map 2, Y4) Roman Barcelona's main temple, now one of the MUHBA heritage sites, was located just behind Plaça Sant Jaume. It was dedicated to the emperor Caesar Augustus in the 1st century. Its four remaining Corinthian columns are hidden away inside an otherwise unassuming building. • Mon 10am–2pm, Tue–Sat 10am–7pm, Sun 10am–8pm ☎ 93 256 21 22 • C/del Paradís 10 ✧ Jaume I

Casa de la Ciutat (map 2, Y4) Facing the Generalitat across Plaça de Sant Jaume, the Ajuntament is Barcelona's City Hall. It has a fairly bland 19th-century neoclassical façade, but like the Generalitat there's an original Gothic one tucked away on C/de la Ciutat. Much of the splendid 14th-century interior is open to the public on Sunday. Reached by a grand staircase, the highlight of the building is the Salò de Cent. This Catalan-Gothic hall dates from 1369, and gets its name from being the place where the Consell de Cent, a government body consisting of 100 representitive citizens from all classes, regulated city affairs from the mid 13th century to the early 1700s. In the courtyard downstairs, look out for sculptures by Joan Miró and Frederic Marès. • Sun 10am–1pm Guided tours in English at 11am ☎ 93 402 70 00 • Plaça de Sant Jaume 1 ✧ Jaume I, Liceu

MIBA – Museu d'Idees i Invents (map 2, Y4) This new museum will appeal to kids, design fans, or anyone who thinks out of the box. Founded by Pep Torres, a local creative, it exhibits inventions and solutions that makes modern life easier. Some objects are downright absurd, but the museum also includes some wonderful examples of industrial design. • Tue–Fri 10am–2pm and 4pm–7pm, Sat 10am–8pm, Sun 10am–2pm ☎ 93 332 79 30 • C/de la Ciutat 7 ✧ Jaume I

Sants Just i Pastor (map 2, Y4) From C/de la Ciutat, turn left onto C/Hércules, which leads to this 14th-century Catalan Gothic church with baroque additions. It stands on a delightful little square that's a haven of peace in this part of town and a good spot for an inner-city picnic. The Gothic fountain here was built in 1367. • Mon–Sat 11am–2pm, 5–9pm (8pm on Tuesday), Sun 10am–1pm ☎ 93 301 74 33 • Plaça Sant Just 1 ✧ Jaume I

La Mercè (map 2, Z5) C/de la Ciutat leads to C/de la Mercè, just back from the waterfront. This area is slightly more run down than the northern Barri

Gòtic; although it was once one of the most fashionable parts of the city, by the early 20th century it had fallen on hard times. This was when the Picasso family lived here—Picasso Senior taught art at the Escola de Belles Artes located in the huge La Llotja building on Passeig Isabel II, while the fledgling artist learnt about life in the tough streets of the district and the brothels of C/d'Avinyó. His first studio was at C/de la Plata 3, now a restaurant. The area is dominated by the baroque bulk of the **Basílica de la Mercè**, which contains Barcelona's most revered image of the Virgin. A couple of blocks west, the attractive **Plaça Duc de Medinaceli** was designed by Francesc Molina, who also built the Plaça Reial. The column and fountain in the middle of the square, honouring a 14th-century Catalan admiral, is the first monument in Barcelona to be made from iron. ✧ Jaume I, Drassanes

La Ribera (map 2, Y2) Beyond busy Via Laietana is the old maritime quarter of La Ribera (in the days before land reclamation, this was the waterfront). Vast tracts of it were knocked down in the 18th century to make way for the Ciu-tadella, built by the Habsburg rulers after the Catalans had sided against Madrid in the War of the Spanish Succession. Fortunately, some of the glories of the old district remain. The streets around its wrought-iron centre-piece, the old **Mercat del Born**—recently converted into a wonderful cultural centre—are dotted with picturesque apartment blocks, most of them recently spruced up in a major campaign to revitalize what was

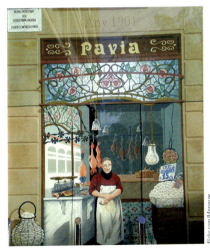

flickr.com/Meneses

once a downtrodden area. The **Carrer de Montcada** is a late-medieval gem, packed with splendid mansions dating back to the 15th century. **El Born** has become the city's hippest place to gallery-hop or simply enjoy a drink on one of its many *terrassas*.
✪ Jaume I, Barceloneta

Museu Picasso (map 2, Z3) Occupying five mansions, the museum has a staggeringly large collection of Picasso's work, with a wealth of paintings, sculpture, ceramics and graphics. It is strongest on three very different phases of the artist's long career—the early years from 1890 till 1904 when Picasso left Barcelona for Paris; his time as a mature Cubist around 1917; and the 1950s, with a large group of canvasses devoted to his intense re-working of Velázquez's *Las Meninas*. Above all, the museum draws out the unstoppable creativity of the man. The early paintings reveal a dazzling precocity. His development from young art student to one of the greatest of modern artists takes place magically before your eyes. The extraordinary ability shown in Realist works such as the self portraits of 1896–97, the portraits of his parents and the assured *First Communion*, is matched only by the ease with which he abandoned all this and re-invented European art at the turn of the 20th century. • Tues–Sun 10am–8pm ☎ 93 256 30 00 • C/Montcada 15–23
✪ Jaume I

El Born Centre Cultural (map 2, Z3) This recently opened cultural centre is a fascinating mix of part archaelogical museum and part architectural relic. In the process of giving El Born's landmark cast iron market a new use, extensive remains of early 17th

◀ A quiet moment in the heart of the old Ribera district.

century Barcelona were discovered in its foundations; in 1714 the city fell to French and Spanish forces and Catalonia's long (and continuing) struggle for independence began. Huge placards explain the story, whilst the ancient urban layout can be viewed from suspended walkways inside the old edifice. • Tues–Sun 10am–8pm ☎ 93 256 68 51 • Plaça Comercial 12 ✦ Jaume I, Arc de Triomf

Museu de la Xocolata (map 2, Z2) The best time to see the chocolate museum is during the weeks preceding Easter, when all the city *pastisserias* display

PENNY WISE

Barcelona is no longer the bargain destination it once was, though it still offers great value for money if you know the tricks. If you're planning a full assault on Barcelona's splendid array of museums and galleries, it's definitely worth purchasing the **Barcelona Card**. This gives 15–100% reductions at all the main sites, as well as offering discounts at selected shops, restaurants, nightclubs and attractions and free public transport. It's available from tourist offices and prices start at 34 € for two days. But also remember that many of Barce-

lona's top museums, including the Museu Picasso (p. 37) and the MUHBA (p. 32) are free on Sunday afternoons after 3pm and also all day on the first Sunday of every month. For other days, you can purchase single tickets for most museums, official tours, the Bus Turístic and other services on the Barcelona Turisme website at discounted rates of 5-25% (www.barcelonaturisme.com).
Eating out is still one of the city's best bargains, especially if you opt for a substantial lunch. *Menu del día* (three courses, plus a glass of wine) generally hover

around the 12 € mark, but many of the city's top eateries (even ones embellished with Michelin stars) offer them for 25-30 €, less than half of what you would pay for an evening sitting. Street food, bar the kebab joints, still fares poorly but the concept of the "picnic" is catching on. You'll see many locals heading to the parks with a sandwich at lunchtime. As for accommodation, try to book ahead as far as possible. Unless your visit coincides with a major event or trade fair you'll be surprised at the deals possible, even for luxury hotels.

their astonishing *monas*: cakes topped with elaborate chocolate sculptures decorated with feathers, jewels and anything else that takes the artist's fancy. The exhibition takes you through the history of chocolate making and samples are for sale in the café • Mon–Sat 10am–7pm **(8pm in the summer)**, Sun 10am–3pm ☎ 93 268 78 78 • C/Comerç 36 ✧ Jaume I

Santa Maria del Mar (map 2, Z4) This superb Catalan-Gothic church at the end of C/de Montada overlooked the sea when building started in 1329. The restrained decor of the interior, with a magnificent 15th-century rose window at the south end, widely spaced Gothic arches and a dramatic fan-vaulted ceiling, is courtesy of Spanish Civil War anarchists, who set fire to the place in 1936. • Mon–Sat 9am–1.30pm, 4.30–8.30pm, Sun 10.30am–4.30pm, 5–8.45pm ☎ 93 319 00 16 • Plaça de Santa Maria ✧ Jaume I

Parc de la Ciutadella (E5) This pleasant park was laid out on the site of the hated Ciutadella: the Habsburg fortress was so big that it took 10 years to pull it down in the mid-19th century. Today, the park contains a boating lake, the City Zoo, a winter garden and an ornamental fountain in neoclassical style, partly worked on by the young Antoni Gaudí. The fairytale-like bulding you see at the northwest corner is named the **Castell dels Tres Dragons** (Castle of the Three Dragons), a witty Modernista parody of a medieval castle by Domènech i Montaner, that once served as the café-restaurant for the 1888 Exposition. (It is currently being refurbished for a future research centre and library). Another relic of the 1888 Universal Exposition lies at the northern entrance—the red-brick **Arc de Triomf**. The Catalonian Parliament is here, too, and occupies a remaining part of the old Ciutadella fort. ✧ Jaume I, Arc de Triomf

MEAM – Museu Europeu d'Art Modern (map 2, Z3) This exciting new museum is housed inside the Palau Gomis, a sumptuous Renaissance palace that has been graciously and sympathetically restored. The collection, which belongs to a private foundation, displays work from predominantly Spanish artists working in the realm of figurative painting and sculpture, a genre often overlooked in modern art museums. Highlights include Iván Carlos Franco Fraga's photo-realistic portraits and the neo-religious compositions of Juan Manuel Cossio. • Tue–Sun 10am–8pm ☎ 93 319 56 93 • C/Barra de Ferro 5 ✧ Jaume I

WALKING TOUR: CIUTAT VELLA

Just off the northern end of La Rambla in the C/de Santa Anna, **Església de Santa Anna** is a beautiful Gothic church with a delightful cloister. Much of the medieval Ciutat Vella sits on the ancient Roman city of Barcino. The first reminder of the original settlers on this walking tour is south of the church on Plaça de la Vila de Madrid, once the site of the ancient **Via Sepulcral Romana**, where a number of excavated tombs can be seen. Continue down to C/de la Portaferrissa, one of the district's liveliest shopping streets, and turn left to reach **Plaça Nova**, near the cathedral. This was the main gateway to Barcino, and at the start of C/del Bisbe, on the south side of the square, are two massive **Roman towers** that originally guarded the entrance to the city, though their appearance was heavily altered in the 19th century. C/del Bisbe cuts a narrow channel between the cathedral and the Palau de la Generalitat, and leads to **Plaça de Sant Jaume**, which has been the heart of the Old Town since its time as the Roman forum. You can reach the four remaining Corinthian columns of the 1st-century **Temple d'August** from C/del Paradis on the north side of the square. Go back across Plaça de Sant Jaume to C/de la Ciutat, next to the Ajuntament (City Hall) and where its original medieval façade can be seen, and turn first left onto C/d'Hercules. Follow this to picturesque **Plaça de Sant Just**, a small gem of a square dominated by the 14th-century **Basílica dels Sants Just i Pastor**, an attractive single-nave Catalan Gothic church with fine stained-glass windows. The **fountain** on the square dates from 1367. For creative Catalan cuisine, grab a drink and a bite to eat on the terrace of the **Cafè de l'Acadèmia**. From the square, turn northwest along the **C/de la Dagueria**, a lane where the feel of medieval Barcelona is tangible, and turn right on C/de Jaume I to C/del Sots-Tinent Navarro. This street traces the outer wall of Barcino and there are some stretches of the **Roman wall** still in place, including a watchtower at the corner of C/Baixada de Caçador (now part of a hotel) and a considerable part incorporated into the Palau Reial to the north, best seen from **Plaça de Ramon Berenguer el Gran**. More than 4,000 sq m of this part of Roman Barcelona is revealed in detail below street level from inside the **Museu d'Història de Barcelona**. From here, it's an easy walk along C/de Jaume I to La Rambla.

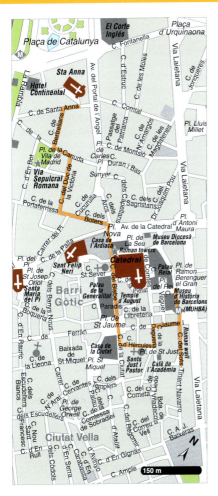

Discover the city's origins, then lose yourself in the warren of medieval alleyways behind the cathedral, where you're sure to find the perfect café or bar to chill out.

Start:
Església de Santa Anna
⬥ Catalunya

Finish:
Museu d'Història de Barcelona
⬥ Jaume I

CHILDREN'S BARCELONA

With its great range of museums, parks and activities, offering everything from funfairs and football to science and sandy beaches, Barcelona will amuse and amaze youngsters whatever their age or interest.

Museums with more

The interactive **CosmoCaixa** science museum, in Zona Alta, invites visitors to prod, play and generally fiddle around with the exhibits, making it a sure-fire winner with kids, while major displays such as the Amazonian rainforest and planetarium are guaranteed to impress.

There are few children who won't enjoy a tour of the **Museu de la Xocolata** in Sant Pere. This isn't just down to the eye-catching chocolate statues and sculptures but also because of the tasting sessions of a product first introduced to the world courtesy of the Spanish.

A visit to the **Museu del FC Barcelona**, located at Barcelona's Camp Nou stadium, is a thrill. There's lots of football memorabilia, and the chance to enter the stadium via the players' tunnel and imagine the roar on match days when you'd be greeted by 100,000 cheering spectators. Many Barcelona museums hold special workshops for children, almost always related to whatever show is on and generally taking place on Saturday or Sunday mornings. The **Centre de Cultura Contemporània (CCCB)** and **Caixa-Forum** are particularly strong on animated and colourful shows and activities. **Poble Espanyol** often hosts puppet and magic shows on the weekends. To find out what's on for the little ones, check out the website: www.kidsinbarcelona.com and www.mammaproof.org (Spanish only).

Pleasure park principle

Perched on the summit of Tibidabo with spectacular views over the city, just the location of the **Tibidabo** amusement park will please children, but they'll love it even more when they see things from the top of the Ferris wheel. The funfair mixes old-fashioned rides with newer, hair-raising attractions such as the freefall Pendulum and has a separate park for small children (called the Camí del Cel), which offers calmer attractions and fabulous views. Check ahead for opening times and transport options.

While not exactly qualifying as theme parks in the usual sense, much of Antonio Gaudí's extravagant work has a magical grip on the imagination of children. Whether it's on the roof of **La Pedrera**, with its army of chimney pots designed to resemble medieval knights in armour, or in **Parc Güell**, filled with squiggly serpentine benches, lizard fountains and fairy-tale gatehouses, they will immediately recognize the fantasyland genius of the Catalan architect.

Fishes and fauna

You can't go wrong with a trip to **L'Aquàrium**, in Port Vell. One of Europe's largest aquariums, it has hundreds of different species of fish from around the world. There can be few children who won't love the unnerving sensation of standing in the 80-m tunnel through the shark tank, surrounded by a swarm of razor-toothed sharks.

Altogether less fishy a place, the **Zoo de Barcelona**, in Parc de la Ciutadella, has tremendous child-appeal, with favourite big beasts like hippos and elephants, a monkey house, dolphin shows, pony rides and a mini-train for getting around on. The park itself has a miniature lake, where rowboats can be hired, and small playgrounds scattered throughout.

Seaside fun

There are plenty of other things to do by the waterfront apart from hanging out on the beach. Youngsters always enjoy messing about in boats, and a trip on one of the *golondrina* pleasure **boat tours** from Port Vell is bound to please. The catamarans have glass bottomed areas.

The vast **Parc del Fòrum** area, future site of a marine zoo, is a great place for kids. The **Museu Blau** on natural sciences is also here, as well as an urban adventure playground.

EL RAVAL

The Raval lies like a mirror-image of the Barri Gòtic on the other side of La Rambla. In the 1920s and 30s the area was known as the Barri Xino, a Chinatown with few Chinese but plenty of exotic lowlife, and the city's raciest red-light district. It's still a place to be careful at night, although time and the efforts of city planners have tamed it. In the backstreets you'll find some of Barcelona's most atmospheric bars and restaurants and a handful of sights that shouldn't be missed.

THE DISTRICT AT A GLANCE

Centre de Cultura Contemporània de Barcelona (CCCB) (C4) This show-piece gallery holds temporary exhibitions of art and architecture, as well as showing films and putting on concerts. The building is a former workhouse and lunatic asylum, and its neoclassical shell is harmoniously juxtaposed with some imaginative modernization and the high-tech arts centre inside. • **Tues–Sun** 11am–8 pm ☎ 93 306 41 00 • C/Montalegre 5 ◈ Catalunya, Universitat

Museu d'Art Contemporani de Barcelona (MACBA) (C4) It rises out of the Raval like a mirage, so shimmering white among the dark old streets that it's almost blinding to look at in the midday sun. Designed by the American architect Richard Meier, the gallery concentrates on trends in international as well as Catalan art since the 1940s. Works on display are drawn from a grow-ing collection and are regularly rotated. Artists to look out for include Miró, Klee

The window displays in El Raval are worth a second look.

and Rauschenberg, and home-grown talent such as Joan Brossa, Miquel Barceló and Susana Solano. The vast square outside the museum is a lively epicentre of the neighbourhood, and a magnet for strollers and skateboarders. • Winter: Mon, Wed–Fri 11am–7.30pm, Sat 10am–9pm, Sun 10am–3pm; Summer: Mon, Wed–Fri 11am–8pm, Sat 10am–8pm, Sun 10am–3pm. Closed on Tuesday. ☎ 93 412 08 10 • Plaça dels Àngels 1 ✛ Catalunya, Universitat

Monestir de Sant Pau del Camp (C5) The squat tower of Barcelona's oldest church, originally built in the 10th century by Benedictines, peeps out from among tall palm trees. The present church is mainly Romanesque in style and dates from the 11th–12th centuries, when the area around here was open fields and earned it the name of St Paul of the Countryside. • Mon–Sat 10am–1.30pm and 4–7.30pm ☎ 93 441 00 01 • C/Sant Pau 101 ✛ Paral.lel

Palau Güell (C–D5) This Unesco–classified mansion was Antoni Gaudí's first mature work, commissioned as a private home by the industrialist Eusebi Güell. Built in 1886–90, it bears the master's trademark touches in every aspect from the basement stables to the rooftop. The highlight is the wavy roof, whose forest of chimneys is decorated with pieces of broken ceramic tiles. This technique, known as *trencadis*, was first brought to Spain by the Arabs and triumphantly revived by Gaudí. After a seven-year renovation period, the interior recently reopened to the public. The audio guide (which is included in the entry fee) explains the building's infamous history—during the Civil War it was used as a prison and anarchist headquarters • **Tues–Sat 10am–8pm (5.30 Nov–March)** ☎ **93 472 57 75** • C/Nou de la Rambla 3–5 ✿ Liceu

Museu Marítim de Barcelona (MMB) (C5) The Maritime Museum is housed in the city's most outstanding Catalan-Gothic secular building, the 13th–14th century Drassanes Reials de Barcelona (Royal Shipyards). Beneath the huge stone-vaulted ceilings, ships were built and sent out to forge Catalonia's maritime empire in the Middle Ages. The building has been recently restored and exhibits inside are scarce, but always on show is the full-size replica, intricately carved and gilded, of the victorious flagship of the Battle of Lepanto (1571), a galley propelled by 48 oars. Outside the entrance, there is a lovely café in the courtyard and a visit to the *Santa Eulàlia* tall ship, moored in the port, is included in the entry fee. • **Daily 10am– 8pm** ☎ **93 342 99 20** • Av. de les Drassanes ✿ Drassanes

A new vocation for a former workhouse: the CCCB.

WALKING TOUR: EL RAVAL

Having set off from the gleaming white MACBA building on Plaça dels Àngels, head west and along C/de Ferlandina to nearby C/de Joaquín Costa. Take note of the **Casa Almirall** at No. 33, an eye-catching Modernista bar that has been serving up cocktails and other alcoholic delights since 1860.

Turn left and walk seawards. The street intersects with C/del Peu de la Creu. To the left is **Satan's Coffee Corner**, a great place for a cup of Java and typical of El Raval's new start-up businesses. Continue along C/del Peu de la Creu until the road intersects with **C/del Doctor Dou**, which contains some of the city's most cutting edge fashion and designs shops. At the southern end of the street is the **Antic Hospital de la Santa Creu**. This early 15th-century Gothic hospital received patients right up to the 1920s—Antoni Gaudí, one of the last of them, died here in 1926. It is now a library, and the colonnaded courtyard has an enjoyable little café and is a nicely shady place to linger for a while.

To the west, along C/de l'Hospital, is **Rambla del Raval**, the district's riposte to the rather larger and more famous Rambla. Until recently a dingy and somewhat down-at-heel corner, it's now lined with palm-trees and sports an increasing number of trendy cafés, like **Madame Jasmine** at No. 22 and **Suculent** at No. 43.

The bottom end of the street runs into C/de Sant Pau. Turn left along this street to reach the Romanesque **Sant Pau del Camp**, the oldest church in Barcelona. South of C/de Sant Pau is the once notorious **Barri Xino**, formerly packed with seedy bars, brothels and cabarets, all of which exerted a powerful attraction on such famous inhabitants as Picasso and Miró. The centre of the action was **C/Nou de la Rambla**, running parallel with C/de Sant Pau, which has been significantly cleaned up in recent times, as is evident when looking at the magnificent **Hotel España**, a Modernista hotel that has been restored to its former, formidable glory; in fact the massive entrance foyer resembles a contemporary art museum (number 9–11).

From here, walk back along C/Nou de la Rambla, passing on the way Gaudí's first masterpiece, the **Palau Güell**. A few steps takes you out of El Raval into La Rambla.

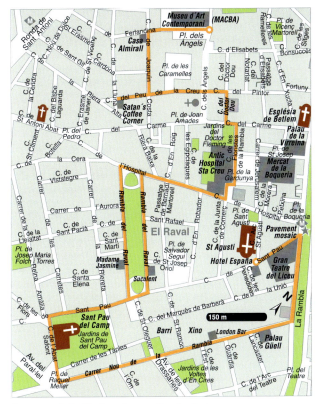

An area packed with atmosphere and local colour.

Start: MACBA building, Plaça dels Àngels ✛ Universitat

Finish: Palau Güell ✛ Liceu

FESTIVAL CITY

Given the liveliness of the city and the irresistible attraction of enjoying life on the street felt by its inhabitants, it can seem like every day is festival day in Barcelona. Curiously, it's not that far from the truth, because the Barcelonans' love of festivals—or *festes*, in Catalonian—means that they are held throughout the year. For visitors, this has the happy result that, should you want to see the city in full festival mode, it's not difficult to find the right time to go.

Winter

Barcelona can get a little chilly in January, but the **Cavalcada de Reis**, the Parade of the Three Kings, held on January 5th, should warm things up. After the Three Kings have arrived by sea and been greeted by the mayor of Barcelona, the parade kicks off. A procession of colourful floats, dancers and loud music is led by the kings, who throw thousands of sweets into the crowd—a symbolic reminder of Epiphany (January 6th), which is traditionally the time when children receive their Christmas presents.

The biggest and brashest winter festival, however, is **Carnestoltes**—better known as Carnaval. This pre-Lenten rave-up—originally the last moment of excess before the forty days of clean living before Easter—involves street parties, costumed processions, marching bands and Brazilian dancers, papier mâché giants and a figure representing King Carnestoltes himself, a Lord of Misrule who presides over the general mayhem. The festival covers the whole of Barcelona and lasts for ten days (a moveable feast, it can occur anytime between early February and mid-March). If you want to see carnival excess taken to the limit, head to nearby Sitges, where the large gay community gives it a twist of outrageous flamboyance.

Spring

La Diada de Sant Jordi, St George's Day, is on April 23rd and celebrates Catalonia's patron saint. It's also the day on which both Cervantes and Shakespeare died in 1616, and it has become traditional to mark the occasion by giving either a red rose or a book as a present, a result of which is that the centre of Barcelona is transformed into a gigantic book and flower market for the day.

In late May, the **Festival de Flamenco de Ciutat Vella** at the Centre de Cultura Contemporània de Barcelona and other venues in Raval is a week long series of concerts and activities that will delight devotees of flamenco.

Summer

The **Trobada Castellera** is a festival of Catalonian physical unity taken to dizzying heights: in June in the Plaça Sant Jaume, teams of *casteller* compete to build the tallest human tower. Accompanied by music, and with the teams dressed in bright red and white outfits, it makes for a striking and curiously thrilling spectacle.

Midsummer brings with it the **Nit de Sant Joan**. The feast day of John the Baptist is celebrated on the night of June 23rd when the Barcelonan sky is lit up by bonfires and fireworks. The largest displays are along the beaches.

From late June through to early August Barcelona hums happily to the **Festival del Grec**, a huge celebration of music, theatre, circus and dance that takes its name from one of the main venues, the open-air Teatre Grec on Montjuïc.

In mid-August, the **Festa Major de Gràcia** is a local festival that's become the biggest summer bash in Barcelona. For one week, the streets of the Gràcia district compete to be the most lavishly decorated, and hold court to parades, parties, concerts, firework displays—and what seems like vineyard-sized quantities of *cava*.

Autumn

The transition from summer to autumn in late September is marked by the **Festes de la Mercè**, a riotous week of human tower-building, folk dancing, *gegant* (giant puppet) parades and the *correfoc*—a procession of fire-spouting, crowd-scaring dragons.

The year of Barcelonan festivals is rounded off with the **Festival Internacional de Jazz** throughout November, bringing in famous names from the world of music. And, in the last couple of weeks before Christmas, there's the popular **Fira de Santa Llúcia**, a Christmas fair specializing in Catalonian craftwork held on the cathedral square.

WATERFRONT

When the advent of container shipping in the 1960s and 70s forced the main port to move to a larger site a short distance along the coast, Barcelona's old port (Port Vell) soon fell into a state of decay. Since then, the transformation of around 3 km of city waterfront—including the creation of a swish harbourside restaurant area for the 1992 Olympic Games—has been little short of miraculous. These days it forms one of the city's liveliest and most extensive entertainment and leisure spots. What's more, there's excellent bathing to be enjoyed just a stone's throw from the city centre.

THE DISTRICT AT A GLANCE

Las Golondrinas (D5) The name means "swallow"—as in the bird. Something of a local institution, the boats have been showing visitors the sights of Barcelona from the water since the 19th century. Shorter harbour tours last 40 minutes or an hour, with alternative routes depending on weather and sea conditions, while the 90-minute sailings skirt the coast as far as the northeast of the city and back. It's always leisurely and relaxing, as well as being a great way to catch a breeze in summer. The departure point is at Portal de la Pau, in front of the Columbus Monument (and from the PortForum in the summer).
• Sailings daily from February to November, depending on weather conditions ☎ 93 442 31 06 • Moll de Drassanes ✛ Drassanes

Frank Gehry's big copper-coloured fish in steel lattice was installed on the Port Olímpic for the 1992 Olympic Games.

Telefèric del Port (C5–D6) This scenic—and slightly hair-raising—cable-car, also called Transbordador Aeri, ride glides above the harbour from the waterfront to Montjuïc. It was put in place for the 1929 Expo, and runs from the Torre de Sant Sebastià, located at the western end of Passeig Joan de Borbó in Barceloneta, before landing at the peak of Montjuïc, lending excellent views over the city and port. • Dec 1–Feb 28 and Oct 28–Dec 31, 11am–5.30pm, March 1–June 2 and Sept 1–Oct 27, 11 am–7pm, June 3–Sept 8, 11 am–8pm ☎ 93 441 48 20 • Passeig Escullera ✛ Barceloneta

L'Aquàrium de Barcelona (D6) Divided into 21 separate aquariums with Mediterranean and tropical tanks, this can rightly claim to be one of the world's best collections of marine life. It's a great place to take the kids, and the 80-m tunnel through the shark tank is sure to prove a favourite. The interactive *Explora!* section has over 50 exhibits where you can discover sea life in the shallow salt water lagoons of the Ebro Delta, the beaches of the Costa Brava and Mediterranean reef communities. Outside, the sea-facing **Maremagnum** shopping mall provides a large outdoor entertainment area for the children. • Daily 9.30am–9pm (weekends and public holidays, June and Sept to 9.30pm); July and August 9.30am–11pm ☎ 93 221 74 74 • Moll d'Espanya, Port Vell ◆ Drassanes, Barceloneta

Museu d'Història de Catalunya (D5) The huge Palau de Mar warehouse sits across the Port Vell harbour. It was converted into a prestige museum devoted to the history of the region at considerable expense and opened in 1996. Starting with the pre-Roman Iberian tribes, it gives a resolutely Catalan's-eye view of events through to modern times, with interactive exhibits that allow you to try on armour, dive into a Civil War air-raid shelter and so on. Finding a good place for refreshments poses little problem. There's a 4th-floor café with a superb terrace overlooking Port Vell, while the harbourside arcades below have a string of good-quality fish restaurants. • Tues, Thurs, Fri, Sat 10am–7pm, Wed 10am–8pm, Sun and holidays 10am–2.30pm ☎ 93 225 47 00 • Palau de Mar, Plaça de Pau Vila 3 ◆ Barceloneta

Barceloneta (D–E6) In front of the Palau de Mar, Barceloneta—"Little Barcelona"—was built in the mid-18th century to a design of the French military engineer Prosper Verboom. He had also been responsible for the construction of the Ciutadella, and this grid of straight-as-a-die streets and tenement housing was intended for the inhabitants of La Ribera who had been displaced by the fortress. With its fin de siècle façades, intimate local cafés and rows of washing hanging out of windows to dry, it has somehow managed to keep its salty, working-class character despite now being one of the most coveted places to live in the city. It justifiably prides itself on possessing excellent seafood restaurants, which are worth bearing in mind if you're heading for a day out on the beaches just beyond ◆ Barceloneta

Edifici Gas Natural (E6) Nothing exemplifies the transformation of Barceloneta into a 21st-century hotspot more than Miralles-Tagliabue's stunning 20-storey tower of glass, complete with a massive adjunct glass building protruding from halfway up. For all its sense of scale, however, the tower's all-round reflection of the sky means that it seems to disappear into transparency,

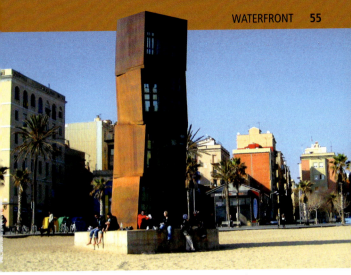

A work of art on the beach: Homenatge a la Barceloneta by German installation artist Rebecca Horn.

much like the natural gas its owners trade in. • **Passeig de Salvat Papasseit** ✧ **Barceloneta**

Port Olímpic (E–F6) The Passeig Marítim beachfront promenade leads from Barceloneta to one the city's most striking modern projects in urban planning. This area was long cut off from the rest of Barcelona by disused factory sites and obsolete railway lines, but it was redeveloped with breathtaking energy and elan in time for the 1992 Olympic Games. Two thousand apartments in the Vila Olímpica were built to house the athletes and a glamorous marina created for the sailing events. The apartments are now privately owned, and the marina is a popular hangout for the Barcelonese, who come here for the bars, nightlife and wall-to-wall fish restaurants. Just back from the marina are two landmark skyscrapers, the Hotel Arts and the Torre Mapfre. The leisure complex next to them has good beachfront restaurants, the Gran Casino and the eye-catching *Peix*, a gigantic steel fish by Frank Gehry. ✧ **Ciutadella-Vila Olímpica**

WALKING TOUR: ALONG THE WATERFRONT

A fitting place to begin any waterfront tour of Barcelona is at the **Monument a Colom**, where La Rambla meets Port Vell (Old Port). This honours the great navigator Christopher Columbus, while behind it to the right is the Drassanes, the medieval shipyards now housing the city's first-rate **Museu Marítim (MMB)**. To your right is the *Santa Eulàlia* tall ship, washed up on Catalan shores in 1919, now restored and forming part of the Museu Marítim's permanent display. The building resembling a ship at the end of the jetty is the World Trade Centre and ferry terminal. Start walking around the port, keeping the water on your right and the Monument a Colom to your left and cross over the undulating **Rambla de Mar footbridge** to the Moll d'Espanya wharf area. Follow the path to the massive **Maremagnum** leisure centre, with its spectacular curving mirror entrance and vast range of shops (also open on Sunday), and on past **L'Aquàrium** (definitely something to return to for a longer visit), a replica of Narcis Monturiol's 19th-century wooden submarine. This loops you round to the **Marina Port Vell**. Phased building development works began here in autumn 2013; once completed, the marina will have 162 fully serviced berths to offer visiting yachts and superyachts. Set off again along the Marina towards the **Palau de Mar** warehouse, containing the excellent **Museu d'Història de Catalunya**. Facing this lies **Barceloneta**, a remarkable working-class neighbourhood of narrow 18th-century streets. Cross **Passeig Joan de Borbó**, lined with enticing fish restaurants (such as El Suquet de l'Almirall at No. 65, which specialises in *suquet*, a type of fish stew) and head along C/Maquinista into the heart of the district. Halfway down on the right is the **Mercat de la Barceloneta**, plastered in solar panels and sheet glass. Go inside for a chance to see Barceloneta's shoppers in full flood. From outside the opposite entrance of the market, cross the square and take any of the streets heading further south. The light at the end of these tunnel-like streets is the glow from the **Platja de Sant Sebastià** beach and the warm Mediterranean sun. Here, you can contemplate the symbolism of *Homenatge a la Barceloneta*, a four-storey sculpture of rusting iron and glass boxes that honours the district. At this point, stretch out on the sand or continue your walk northeast along the promenade to Port Olímpic.

Around the harbours and the beach.

Start:
Monument a Colom
✧ Drassanes

Finish:
Homenatge a la Barceloneta
✧ Barceloneta

MONTJUÏC

The large hill west of the city centre was for centuries used by the military because of its natural strategic advantages, and on more than one occasion the armies of the Madrid kings bombarded the citizens of Barcelona from its heights to keep them in line. Earlier, the Romans had a temple here, and there was a medieval Jewish cemetery, leading to a debate as to whether Montjuïc's name comes from "Mount of the Jews" or "Mount Jove". It has never been a residential area, and there are few cafés or restaurants. But it is home to some of Barcelona's best museums and most scenic viewpoints. The climb up is steep. You can choose easier options such as the funicular (Telefèric), the bus from Plaça d'Espanya, the Bus Turístic or a series of escalators at the foot of the Palau Nacional, home to the MNAC Museum.

THE DISTRICT AT A GLANCE

Castell de Montjuïc (B6) The Castell is at the southern end of Montjuïc, overlooking both town and sea. Dating from the 17th century, it has a bloody history as the place where Barcelona's radicals were tortured and executed, from the anti-Bourbon rebels of the War of the Spanish Succession right up to the Civil War republicans of the 1930s. Until recently, the castle held a collection of military memorabilia, but plans are now underway to turn the complex into an

From the castle walls at the top of Montjuïc you can look over the harbour.

education and information centre on the castle itself and on the surrounding landscape. In the meantime, it's a great place to wander around and take in the spectacular views. During the summer the castle hosts a popular open-air cinema. • Oct–end March daily 10am–6pm, rest of the year 10am–8pm ☎ 93 256 44 45 • Parc de Montjuïc ◈ Paral.lel, then Funicular and Telefèric de Montjuïc (cable car), or 150 bus from Plaça Espanya

Fundació Joan Miró (B5) This beautiful modern gallery was custom-built in the 1970s to display the works of local boy, Joan Miró (1893–1983). The collection gathers together paintings, sculptures and tapestries from all periods of the artist's long life, and provides an unrivalled opportunity to encounter Miró's special blend of the surreal and the abstract. There's also a small group of works by Miró's contemporaries such as Henry Moore, Matisse and Alexander Calder, whose *Mercury Fountain* sculpture was first shown at the Republican pavilion alongside Picasso's *Guernica* during the Paris Exhibition of 1937. • July–Sept

Mirj Blaser

◄ *Joan Miró, Femmes et oiseaux dans la nuit (Women and birds at night), 1967.*

Tues–Sat, 10am–8pm, Thurs 10am–9.30pm, Sun 10am–2.30pm; Oct–June, Tues–Sat 10am–7pm, Thurs 10am–9.30pm, Sun, 10am–2.30pm ☎ 93 443 94 70 • Plaça Neptú, Parc de Montjuïc ◈ Paral.lel, then Funicular, or Bus 55 or 150

Refugi 307 (C5) This old air raid shelter, one of the 1400 that once occupied subterranean Barcelona, is carved into the rocky base of Montjuïc. Its 200 meters of tunnels once protected locals from air raids during the Civil War; a fascinating visit • **Guided tours 10.30am, 11.30am and 12.30pm by appointment** ☎ 93 256 22 00 • Nou de la Rambla 169 ◈ Paral.lel

Museu d'Arqueologia (B5) The archaeological museum is located in one of the buildings on Montjuïc erected for the 1929 Exhibition. Displays of objects found mainly in Catalonia include items from the Greek, Roman and Visigoth eras; there's also a section with Carthaginian jewellery and sculpture discovered in the Balearic Islands. • Tues–Sat 9.30am–7pm, Sun 10am–2.30pm ☎ 93 423 21 49 • Passeig de Santa Madrona 39–41 ◈ Poble Sec, Espanya

Anella Olímpica (Olympic Ring) (A5) Behind a huge neoclassical façade, the **Estadi Olímpic** was built for the 1929 Exhibition, and then revamped for the 1992 Olympic Games. It is now used for large musical events. Nearby are the Olympic venues of **Palau Sant Jordi** and **Picornell Pools** • Bus 13, 55, 125 and 150

Museu Nacional d'Art de Catalunya (MNAC) (B4–5) You will have had glimpses of the Palau Nacional from all around Montjuïc. Its elaborate spires and domes give it the appearance of a grand Habsburg palace that has been transported here by mistake from Castile; in fact, it's a neo-baroque pastiche, thrown up for the 1929 Exhibition and intended for demolition once the party was over. The building won a reprieve, and today it houses a marvellous collection covering a millennium, through the Romanesque, Gothic and Renaissance periods to the fanciful decorative art and objects of the 19th century Modernista era. The undoubted highlight is the Romanesque section. This splendid group of altar paintings and frescoes were rescued early in the 20th century from churches in the Catalan Pyrenees, where they were falling into decay. Their stylized Romanesque figures with elongated faces both pre-date and transcend a naturalistic approach to painting—and the effect in, for example, the 12th-century fresco of *Christ Pantocrator* from the church of Sant Climent de Taüll, is overwhelmingly powerful and direct. The Gothic collection pales a little in comparison, though works by artists such as Bernat Martorell (1400–52) and Jaume Huguet (1412–92)—note his exquisite *St George and the Princess*—more than justify the claim that this was a Golden Age of Catalonian culture. The **Thyssen Collection** is a small but important bequest of medieval, Renaissance and baroque works from central and southern Europe. The undisputed jewel is the bewitching *Madonna of*

Virgin and Child by Peter Paul Rubens at the MNAC. ▶

Humility (1435) by Fra Angelico. The other new collection, the Modern Art section, holds pieces from Catalonia's Modernista period; fine sculpture, painting and decorative arts (including furniture by Gaudí), many of which graced the stately homes of the city's bourgeoisie in the late 19th century. Look for the painting *Ramon Casas and Pere Romeu on a Tandem*, an iconic work of the period that once hung in the café Els Quatre Gats. • Oct–April Tues–Sat 10am–6pm, May–Sept 10am–8pm; Sun 10am–3pm ☎ 93 622 03 76 • Palau Nacional, Parc de Montjuïc ✦ Espanya, then escalator

Font Màgica de Montjuïc (B4) The "magic" fountain, directly in front of the MNAC, is another amazing relic of the 1929 Exhibition and said to be the only one of its kind in the world. During a performance (sometimes with music), smoke-like sprays of water and jets like fireworks are lit by pink, turquoise, red and white lights. • Oct–end April Fri–Sat 7pm–9pm, May–end Sept, Thurs–Sun 9pm–11.30pm • Plaça d'Espanya ✦ Espanya

CaixaForum (B4) This small, select collection of contemporary art is housed in a magnificent Modernista building, the Casaramona designed by Puig i Cadalfach. The permanent collection includes works by LeWitt, Schnabel and other international and Spanish artists of the calibre of Tàpies. Temporary shows can range from a study of the German Bauhaus movement to masterpieces from the Italian Renaissance. The building itself, an old textile factory, has been magnificently renovated, with a new main entrance designed by Japanese architect Arata Isozaki. Concerts are held on its patios during the summer months, and there are many other activities including lectures and literary events. • Mon–Fri 10am–8pm, Sat, Sun 10am–9pm, Wed July–Aug 10am–11pm ☎ 93 476 86 00 • Av. Francesc Ferrer i Guàrdia 6–8 ✦ Espanya

Pavelló Mies van der Rohe (B4) Made of glass, steel and four different kinds of marble, the German contribution to the 1929 Exhibition by Ludwig Mies van der Rohe (1886–1969) was designed to accommodate the official reception. It was disassembled after the Exhibition but reconstructed on the same site in 1986 as witness to its architectural significance. The pavilion's hard purity of line and relentless rationalism was the way of the future when it was first built, and marked a radical departure from Barcelona's vertiginous

Just water and light, but the Font Màgica draws admiring crowds every night.

and wavy Modernista style. Free tours in English on Saturdays at 10am. • **Open daily 10am–8pm** ☎ 93 423 40 16 • Av. Francesc Ferrer i Guàrdia 7 ◆ Espanya

Poble Espanyol (A4) The road next to the pavilion leads up to this adjunct to the 1929 Exhibition, a "Spanish Village" exemplifying traditional architectural styles from around the country. Enter through a replica of the 12th-century gates of Àvila to the Plaça Mayor, the main square with a mix of mock-medieval and Renaissance buildings from Castile and Aragon. Beyond here are winding streets with Andalusian churches, Zaragozan towers and houses from every Spanish region, inhabited by craft and souvenir shops, bars and restaurants, dance clubs and even a small museum of Catalan art. • **Mon 9am–8pm, Tues–Thurs and Sun 9am–midnight, Fri 9am–3am, Sat 9am–4am** (times vary for shops, restaurants and other attractions; an extra entry fee maybe required for these) ☎ 93 508 63 00 • Av. Francesc Ferrer i Guàrdia 13 ◆ Espanya

WALKING TOUR: MONTJUÏC

You might want to pop into the dazzling **Fundació Joan Miró** for a quick look at the master's famous artistic squiggles or to sip a *cafè amb llet* (a Catalonian latte) on the terrace before continuing along Avinguda de Miramar. At the **Estació Parc Montjuïc**, hop onto a Telefèric cable car and conserve energy on the ascent to the **Castell de Montjuïc**. If you are still feeling fit after doing a lap of the castle's battlements, work your way across the hill along the Passeig del Migdía, which leads to the **Cementiri del Sud-oest** (follow the signs), a vast and varied 19th-century cemetery. Alternatively take Carrer del Foc heading in a westerly direction from the castle and turn right into C/de Can Valero. You will pass the lovely **Jardí Botànic** on your left and on the right will be the **Jardí Petra Kelly**, dedicated to the German politician assassinated in 1992. Turn left at the C/del Doctor Font i Quer and continue to the intersection of the Passeig Olímpic. Here is the **Estadi Olímpic**, the centre stage of the Barcelona's 1992 Olympic Games. Loop around the stadium to the Avinguda l'Estadi and the **Museu Olímpic i de l'Esport** (at No. 60), which covers the history of sport in general and of the Olympics in particular. Further eastwards and on the left, is Plaça d'Europa where the slim, white **Torre Calatrava** tilts elegantly into the sky. Take the escalators in front of the Piscines Bernat Picornell and then wind your way downhill to arrive in front of the MNAC Museum. Continue downhill until you reach the Avinguda Francesc Ferrer i Guàrdia. Here, the **Poble Espanyol**, a faux Spanish village built for the 1929 World Exhibition, has cafés and restaurants among the shops. In front of the **Pavelló Mies van der Rohe** is the **CaixaForum**, a stunning modern arts complex converted from an old textile factory. Continue northwards to **Plaça d'Espanya** with its **Torres Venecianes** which marked the entrance to the 1929 exhibition. There's no better way to end a walking tour of this area than with drinks and tapas. Try **La Lola**, one of the handful of bars and restaurants on the roof of the **Arenas**, an old bullring converted to a shopping centre (Gran Via de les Corts Catalanes 373–385). If you still have some energy, you could cross the Gran Via and turn right into C/Llerída. Take any left street and you will find yourself in **Poble Sec**—a charming *barri* with pretty cafés and squares alongside inexpensive bars and restaurants.

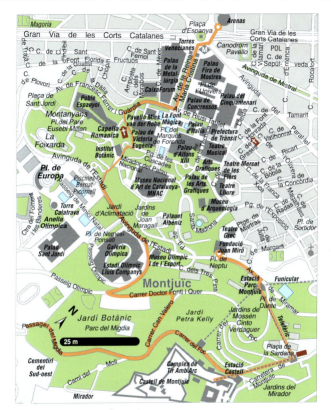

A long walk with magnificent views.

Start: Fundació Joan Miró (bus 55 or 150); for a shorter walk, start at the Estadi Olímpic

Finish: Plaça d'Espanya ✧ Espanya

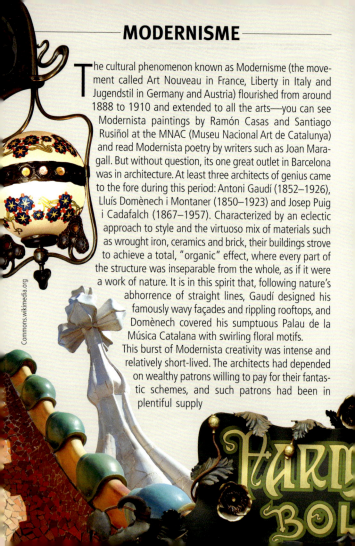

MODERNISME

The cultural phenomenon known as Modernisme (the movement called Art Nouveau in France, Liberty in Italy and Jugendstil in Germany and Austria) flourished from around 1888 to 1910 and extended to all the arts—you can see Modernista paintings by Ramón Casas and Santiago Rusiñol at the MNAC (Museu Nacional Art de Catalunya) and read Modernista poetry by writers such as Joan Maragall. But without question, its one great outlet in Barcelona was in architecture. At least three architects of genius came to the fore during this period: Antoni Gaudí (1852–1926), Lluís Domènech i Montaner (1850–1923) and Josep Puig i Cadafalch (1867–1957). Characterized by an eclectic approach to style and the virtuoso mix of materials such as wrought iron, ceramics and brick, their buildings strove to achieve a total, "organic" effect, where every part of the structure was inseparable from the whole, as if it were a work of nature. It is in this spirit that, following nature's abhorrence of straight lines, Gaudí designed his famously wavy façades and rippling rooftops, and Domènech covered his sumptuous Palau de la Música Catalana with swirling floral motifs.

This burst of Modernista creativity was intense and relatively short-lived. The architects had depended on wealthy patrons willing to pay for their fantastic schemes, and such patrons had been in plentiful supply

Commons.wikimedia.org

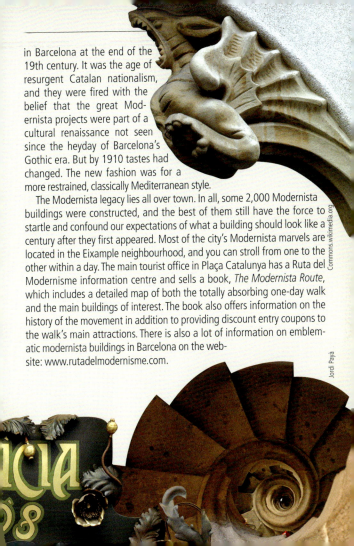

in Barcelona at the end of the 19th century. It was the age of resurgent Catalan nationalism, and they were fired with the belief that the great Modernista projects were part of a cultural renaissance not seen since the heyday of Barcelona's Gothic era. But by 1910 tastes had changed. The new fashion was for a more restrained, classically Mediterranean style.

The Modernista legacy lies all over town. In all, some 2,000 Modernista buildings were constructed, and the best of them still have the force to startle and confound our expectations of what a building should look like a century after they first appeared. Most of the city's Modernista marvels are located in the Eixample neighbourhood, and you can stroll from one to the other within a day. The main tourist office in Plaça Catalunya has a Ruta del Modernisme information centre and sells a book, *The Modernista Route*, which includes a detailed map of both the totally absorbing one-day walk and the main buildings of interest. The book also offers information on the history of the movement in addition to providing discount entry coupons to the walk's main attractions. There is also a lot of information on emblematic modernista buildings in Barcelona on the website: www.rutadelmodernisme.com.

Commons.wikimedia.org

Jordi Payà

EIXAMPLE AND GRÀCIA

Until the 1860s, Barcelona was restricted by the Madrid government from any expansion outside the city walls, and the land north of the old town was almost completely open country, with just an ancient dirt track leading up to the small village of Gràcia and the hills beyond. But a period of liberal rule under Isabel II saw the restrictions lifted and the face of Barcelona changed forever. The successful plan for the city's extension (*eixample*, in Catalan) was the work of Ildefons Cerdà, who came up with the vast geometrical pattern of grids, axes roads and boulevards that, by and large, became the Eixample we know today. Its relentless blocks are relieved by the presence of the best of Modernista architecture and Gaudí's final, incomplete masterpiece, the Sagrada Família church. Meanwhile, the district of Gràcia retains its village atmosphere, and a number of small squares, popular bars and restaurants make it a great place simply to wander around and explore.

THE DISTRICTS AT A GLANCE

Plaça de Catalunya (D4) This massive square marks the border between the old town and the Eixample. Completed only in the 1920s, it is now the hub around which the city revolves—metro, FGC and mainline trains, airport and

In Passeig de Gràcia you can feel Modernisme beneath your feet.

tourist buses all stop here, and it contains the main tourist information office. It is lined by a fairly uninspiring array of monumental buildings (one, on the corner of Pg de Gràcia, houses an Apple store), though the **El Corte Inglés** department store is not only a useful landmark but also a good place for one-stop shopping and has a great supermarket in the basement. **El Triangle** at No. 4 is an enormous shopping complex with branches of FNAC, the beauty product megastore Sephora and other specialty shops. ◈ Catalunya

Passeig de Gràcia (D4) The old road to Gràcia underwent a remarkable metamorphosis when the Eixample was built, and it was re-invented as one of Europe's finest boulevards. Broad, tree-lined and with a range of pavement cafés to stop at, it's a superb place to walk. From the Gran Via to Avinguda Diagonal at the northern end, are a host of chic boutiques and smart jewellery shops, while the Manzana de la Discórdia and la Pedrera buildings have the most concentrated burst of Modernista creativity anywhere in the city. At No.

96, the department store **Vinçon** contains two floors of the best home, garden and officeware, and has been prominent in promoting Barcelona as a "design" city. Even if you can't abide shops, look at the window displays, worth the trip alone. ✤ Catalunya, Passeig de Gràcia

Manzana de la Discòrdia (D3) The name given to the block just before C/d'Aragó is a pun on Block or Apple of Discord, because of the fantastic incongruity of three of its buildings. They were designed by the three leading Catalan Modernista architects, and stand as a microcosm of the whole movement. Note that unrestricted access is only available into the Casa Batlló (see entry below). At No. 35, on the corner of C/de Consell de Cent, is Domènech i Montaner's **Casa Lleó i Morera**. Dating from 1905, it has a highly embellished façade and Moorish-influenced turrets.

The **Casa Amatller** is a couple of doors up at No. 41, designed by Puig i Cadafalch for a chocolate manufacturer named Antoni Amatller in 1898. The striking stepped gable is a gesture towards Flemish Renaissance style, though the exuberant use of polychrome ceramic tiles is pure Catalan Modernisme. The building houses the Institute of Hispanic Art. It can be viewed, by prior arrangement, on Saturday mornings. • **Passeig de Gràcia 35–43** ☎ **93 216 01 75** (Casa Amatller) ✤ Passeig de Gràcia

Casa Batlló (D3) Looking like one of Mr Amatller's colourful confections that has been left in the sun, Gaudí's more immediately eye-catching Casa Batlló (1906) ostentatiously trumps its two neighbours. The leitmotif of the work is the legend of St George (patron saint of Catalonia). Various entry options give you access to the sinuous staircase, the upper roof and spectacular first floor. • **Daily 9am–9pm (also night visits during the summer)** ☎ **93 216 03 06** • **Passeig de Gràcia 43** ✤ Passeig de Gràcia

Fundació Antoni Tàpies (D3) Take the first turning left to this gallery dedicated to the renowned Catalan painter and sculptor Antoni Tàpies (1923–2012). This recently renovated former publishing house was built by Domènech i Montaner in 1880, and the red-brick façade is topped by a Tàpies sculpture, titled *Cloud and Chair*, that resembles an enormous piece of barbedwire. It is in fact typical of his work, which is experimental, bold and often polit-

The sandstone pillars on the central window of Casa Batlló look like bones.

ical—much of the early period is explicitly anti-Franco. The gallery also holds temporary exhibitions by other modern artists. • **Tues–Sun 10am–7pm** ☎ **93 487 03 15** • **C/d'Aragó 255** ◈ **Passeig de Gràcia**

Fundació Francisco Godia (D4) This engaging collection has been amassed by Francisco Godia, a successful businessman, racing driver and patron of the arts. Housed in a fanciful modernista mansion (a work of Enric Sagnier, one of the most prolific of the Eixample's architects) it focuses principally on the important Catalan artistic movements; Romanic, Gothic, Art Nouveau and Noucentista. Contemporary art gets a look in too (the collection was expanded by Godia's daughter after he died in 1990) with works by Miquel Barceló, Picasso and Tápies. Each piece has been exquisitely chosen and the collection is beautifully curated. The children's art workshops, generally held on Saturday mornings, are considered to be the best in the city. • **Mon–Sat 10am–8pm, Sun 10am–3pm** ☎ **93 272 31 80** • **C/Diputació 250** ◈ **Catalunya**

Museu del Modernisme Català (D3) The trove of a private collection has been put on display here, with exhibits of furniture, paintings and even jewellery from Barcelona's prolific Modernist period. Standouts include cabinets from the marquetry masters Joan Busquets and Gasper Homer. • Mon–Sat 10am–8pm, Sun 10am–2pm ☎ 93 272 28 96 • C/Balmes 48 ◆ Passeig de Gràcia

A PERMANENT WAVE

At the start of the 20th century, a Barcelona property developer, Pere Milà i Camps, decided to build a new apartment block in the Eixample. A born dandy, he'd recently swept a rich widow, Roser Guardiola, off her feet. Along with a vast fortune, she also brought to the marriage a large plot of land at the corner of Passeig de Gràcia and C/del Provença, which is where Milà planned to put the new block. The joke doing the rounds in Barcelona at the time asked whether he was more excited by the *viuda de Guardiola*, Guardiola's widow, or the *guardiola de la viuda*, the widow's cash box. It was only to be expected that a man so aware of the beneficial effects of style and pizzazz should choose the most dazzling architect in Barcelona to build it for him.

Antoni Gaudí spent four years, from 1906 to 1910, working on the Casa Milà, as it became known, and though the result was suitably extraordinary—in Salvador Dalí's words, a "delirious" and "edible" beauty—it didn't entirely fulfil Milà's original concept. A visionary of the motor age and a man who loved luxury cars, Milà wanted an interior double spiral ramp so that his tenants on the top floors could drive up to and down from their front doorsteps. Unfortunately, the wide turning-circle of their long-bonneted Rolls-Royces and Daimlers and the dangerously steep ramps that would have been necessary ruled this luxury out. Instead, the building got an underground car park—the first in Barcelona—and the pedestrian ramp you can see today.

There's no other church in the world like the Sagrada Família; it's impossible not to be moved by it.

La Pedrera (D3) This is one of Gaudí's best-known buildings. From the wavy façade to the tangled iron railings stuck onto the balconies like so many lumps of seaweed, there doesn't seem to be a straight line on show. Gaudí designed it as an apartment block for the wealthy developer Pere Milà and it is officially called Casa Milà. La Pedrera, meaning "The Stone Quarry", is a less-than-respectful descriptive nickname given to it by Barceloneses. You can take a lift up to the **Espai Gaudí** in the attic, with information about the architect's work, then climb up to the great, undulating roof, whose flamboyant chimneys and ventilators, like otherworldly visitors, have had as much artistic attention lavished on them as any other part of the building. In summer, the roof plays stage to a series of concerts, from salsa to jazz. Check at the ticket office. On the fourth floor, the **Pis de la Pedrera** is a reconstruction of how a Modernista-style apartment would have looked at the start of the 20th century; temporary shows from major artists are held on the first floor. • Daily 9am–6.30pm Nov–Feb, rest of the year 9am–8pm ☎ 90 220 21 38 • Passeig de Gràcia 92 ✪ Diagonal

Temple Expiatori de la Sagrada Família (E3) Work on the Church of the Holy Family began in 1882, but within two years the architect had resigned and the project was taken over by Antoni Gaudí. He worked on it till his death more than 40 years later, at which time it was still far from complete. In many ways, this building can be seen as an important affirmation of the continuing influence of Catalan Gothic in Barcelona with familiar pointed Gothic arches, rose windows and immense spires. Yet nothing is quite as it seems. Look again and you'll see the spires are topped with frilly, multi-coloured flowers and the pinnacles erupt into bunches of fruit. The Nativity Façade on the east side was the one Gaudí mostly worked on; the western entrance is through the Passion Façade, added since the 1950s. The crypt contains a museum devoted to the construction, the towers lend fabulous views of the city. Pope Benedict XVI consecrated the temple in late 2010, paving the way for mass to be held underneath its now-completed main nave. The pre-purchase of tickets through www.sagradafamilia.org is advisable • Daily Apr–Sept 9am–8pm; Oct–Mar 9am–6pm ☎ 93 513 20 60 • Plaça Sagrada Família–C/Mallorca 401 ✪ Sagrada Família

Antic Hospital de la Santa Creu i Sant Pau (F2) From the north end of the church, tree-lined Avinguda Gaudí leads up to another Modernista masterpiece, Domènech i Montaner's hospital complex, begun in 1900. It is the only Modernista building to rival the Sagrada Família in terms of size and scope. There are 48 individual pavilions, each decorated with mosaics and murals. Unfortunately, they proved unsuitable for the demands of modern medicine and new hospital facilities have been built on the same grounds. The complex has recently been extensively and masterfully renovated with many pavilions being converted into research and learning centres. However some, such as the Administrative and St. Jordi pavilions, can be visited by the public, as can the grounds. • Mon–Sat 10–4.30pm (6.30pm April–Oct) Sun 10–2.30pm • Tours in English at 10 am, 12pm, 1pm, 4pm ☎93 553 78 01 • C/de Sant Antoni Maria Claret 167 ✪ Guinardó – Hospital de Sant Pau

Gràcia (D–E1–2) This once separate village long resisted absorption by Barcelona, a fate that was only sealed as recently as 1897, and its charming streets and squares still give the sense of being in another town. **Plaça de la**

Vila de Gràcia is the former town square, with a tall clocktower, town hall and a number of outdoor cafés. From here, you can head straight up to **Plaça del Sol**, a lively spot. Then make your way past the eclectic shops and galleries on the Calle Verdi northeastwards to the **Plaça de la Virreina**, which is graced with the 17th-century church of Sant Josep. To the northeast, **Plaça de Rovira i Trias** is named after the architect whose plans for the Eixample were rejected. A bronze statue of him sits forlornly on a bench. On C/de les Carolines, you'll see the unmistakable imprint of Gaudí's genius on the façade of the **Casa Vicens**. It's a relatively restrained early work of 1883–88, though the Moorish-influenced tiling and wrought-iron fence are exuberant. ✪ Joanic, Fontana

Parc Güell (E1) When Eusebi Güell bought a large tract of hillside north of Gràcia with the intention of developing it as a garden city, he employed Gaudí who began work on it in 1900, landscaping the park and designing the entrance and main public areas. However, the project collapsed, due to a lack of buyers willing to purchase any of the plots. Perhaps what Gaudí had come up with was too advanced for its time—the entrance pavilions are like fairy-tale gingerbread houses. Steps lead from here to the ceramic-encrusted lizard fountain, beyond which is a temple of 84 drunken columns. These support the park's centrepiece, an amazing "terrace in wonderland" edged with a vast, continuous bench, covered in *trencadis*, or broken tiles. The **Casa-Museu Gaudí**, on the western side, is the architect's old home and can be visited for a separate fee. The city bought Güell's folly in 1922 and opened it to the public as a park, although to reduce visitor numbers and damage, it now entails an entry fee. • Daily Oct 27–Mar 23, 8.30am–6.30pm, March 24–April 20, 8am–8pm, May 1–Oct 26, 8am–9.30pm • C/d'Olot ✪ Lesseps or Bus H6, 24, 32, 92

Museu del Disseny de Barcelona (F4) At the end of 2014, the imposing DHUB building became the city's new design museum, showing ceramic and costume collections as well as modern industrial design. It is the centrepiece of the present development around the Glòries area, which includes the new metal canopied home for Els Encants fleamarket (opposite) and Jean Nouvel's soaring Torre Agbar, soon to become a hotel. • Tues–Sun 10am–8pm ☎ 93 256 68 00 • Plaça de les Glòries Catalanes 37–38 ✪ Glòries

WALKING TOUR: EIXAMPLE

For your first contact with Eixample's rich stock of Modernista architecture, head north from Plaça de Catalunya along Passeig de Gràcia, taking a right turn onto C/Casp. No. 48, the **Casa Calvet**, is Gaudí's first apartment block. The ground-floor restaurant offers the chance to see some of the master's classic touches in its stained glass, tiling and wood panelling. From here, walk up C/Roger de Llúria to Gran Via de Les Corts Catalanes and wallow in the Modernista luxury of the **Palace Barcelona** hotel at No. 668, famed for its stylish afternoon tea in the Grand Hall. Return two blocks and turn right onto Passeig de Gràcia, the backbone of the district. A short distance up on the left is **Manzana de la Discòrdia**, a trio of buildings on the same block that form a concentrated introduction to the work of the three greatest Modernista architects: Domènech i Montaner's Moorish-influenced **Casa Lleó i Morera** at No. 35; at No. 41, the **Casa Amatller** by Puig i Cadafalch; and trumping the lot for Modernista extravagance, Gaudí's **Casa Batlló** at No. 43. Take the next left onto C/d'Arago. The **Fundació Antoni Tàpies** is located in Domènech i Montaner's striking, 1880s red-brick structure, the city's first Modernista building. Turn right onto **Rambla de Catalunya**, an attractive tree-lined street with numerous shops, bars and cafés, such as **Mauri** (No. 102), famous for its pastries. Have a peek at the decor in **Farmàcia Bolós** at No. 77. Head right along C/de Provença. On the other side of Passeig de Gràcia is Gaudí's extraordinary **La Pedrera**, whose wavy façade and wonderland rooftop was completed in 1910. Carry on up Passeig de Gràcia, going right at C/del Rosselló. On Avinguda Diagonal, just around the corner to the right, is Puig i Cadafalch's **Palau Baró de Quadras** ornamented with stained glass and neo-Gothic carvings. On the opposite side, at No. 420, is the Casa Terrades, whose nickname of **Casa de les Punxes**—the "House of Spikes"—stems from architect Puig i Cadafalch's plethora of neo-Gothic spires and pinnacles on the façade. From here, head northeast along Av. Diagonal to Passeig Sant Joan, and the same architect's **Palau Macaya** at No. 108, its stunning white frontage embellished by sculptures by leading Modernista artist Eusebi Arnau. Head east along C/de Provença to finish at the **Sagrada Família**.

Carrer de la Marina · Pl. de Gaudí · Pl. de la Hispanitat · Arenas · Carrer de · la · Marina
Sagrada Família · Pl. de Valéncia · Pl. de Pablo Neruda · Jardins de Clotilde Cerdà · de Casp · Carrer d'Ausiàs Marc
Carrer de Rosselló · Carrer de Sardenya · Pl. de la Sagrada Família · Carrer · de · Sardenya · Ribes
Carrer de Corsega · Carrer · de · C. de Provença · C. de Mallorca · Sicília · Avinguda Diagonal · Carrer · de · Diputació · Carrer · de · Sicília · Carrer d'Ausiàs Marc
C. de Nàpols · Carrer d'Aragó · del Consell de Cent · de · C. · de Nàpols
C. Roger de Flor · Jardins del Carlit · N · C. Roger de Flor
Casa Macaya · Museu Egipci · Sant Francesc de Sales · Pl. de Tetuan · 300 m
Passeig de Sant Joan · Pl. de Mossèn Jacint Verdaguer · Passeig · Jardins del Doctor Robert · de Sant Joan
C. de Ballèn · Corts Catalanes · C. de Bailèn
Eixample
C. de Girona · Jardins de la Torre de les Aigües · C. de Girona · C. d'Ausiàs Marc
C. del Bruc · Purísima Concepció · C. del Bruc · Casa Calvet
Casa de les Punxes · de les · Palace Barcelona
C. de Roger Llúria · Museu Egipci · Carrer d'Aragó · del Consell de Cent · Corts · Roger · Llúria · Pl. d'Urquinaona
Carrer de Pau Claris · Gran Via · de · Carrer de Casp · Carrer de Pau de Claris
Palau Baró de Quadras · de Valéncia · Catalanes · Ronda de Sant Pere
Plaça de Joan Carles I · La Pedrera (Casa Milà) · Passeig · de · Casa Amatller · Casa Lleó Morera · Jardins de Maria Callas · Gràcia · El Corte Inglés · C. de Fontanella
Mauri · Casa Batlló · Fundació Antoni Tàpies · Manzana de la Discòrdia · Museu del Perfum · Jardins de la Reina Victoria · Plaça de Catalunya · Ronda de la Universitat
Rambla · de · C. de Provença · C. de Mallorca · de · Farmàcia Bolós · Catalunya · Fundació Francisco Godia

An embarrassment of Modernista riches.

Start: Plaça de Catalunya ✛ Catalunya

Finish: Sagrada Família ✛ Sagrada Família

AROUND BARCELONA

Spread out just beyond the city centre are some of Barcelona's most enjoyable sights. Getting to them is often half the fun, and you'll need to use the full range of public transport, including trains, buses, funicular railways and a picturesque ancient tram system.

THE DISTRICT AT A GLANCE

Museu del Futbol Club Barcelona (A1–2) The seriousness with which Barcelonians take their football can be seen in the sheer scale of Camp Nou, the local team's ground. Seating 120,000 people, it's the largest in Europe. FC Barcelona—known to its fans as Barça—is one of the great names in world football, and this museum, inaugurated in 1984 and recently expanded to include lots of multimedia displays. You'll see team trophies and vast quantities of other football memorabilia. Entry includes a visit to the stadium itself but may be restricted on match days. • Times vary throughout the year, but generally Mon–Sat 10am–6.30 pm (7.30pm summer), Sun 10am–2.30pm (7.30pm summer). Check www.fcbarcelona.es for details (last entry an hour before closing). ☎ 90 218 99 00 • Camp Nou, Av. Arístides Maillol ✛ Collblanc

Parc de Pedralbes (A1) This park provides some leafy, tranquil respite from traffic-filled Diagonal Avenue. It once formed part of the country estate belong-

Cheering on the Champions League winners: Barça colours on one cheek, the Catalan flag on the other.

ing to Eusebi Güell (Gaudí's main patron) and the old gate houses and stables can be viewed by accessing a separate entrance around the corner on Avingu- da Pedrables. The early 20th-century Palau Reial in the centre of the park has served as both Güell's summer home and the Barcelona residence of General Francisco Franco. • **Palau Reial de Pedralbes, Av. Diagonal 686** ✛ **Palau Reial**

Pavellons Güell (A1) Inspired by the Greek legend of Hesperides (and its mythical garden) the stunning wrought iron gate features the Dragon of Pedralbes, an enormous hissing lizard that stands guard over the estate's entrance. The old stables and porter's lodge behind were some of Gaudí's ear- lier works, when he was influenced by the colour and forms of Arabic architec- ture. • **Guided visits only: Sat–Sun 10.15am (English), 11.15am (Catalan), 12.15pm (English) and 1.15pm (Spanish)** ☎ **93 256 25 04** • **Av. de Pedralbes 7** ✛ **Palau Reial**

Tibidabo (map 3) The fun starts with the old Tramvia Blau ("Blue Tram") that rattles you along to the funicular station for the steep ride up Tibidabo. At 542 m, this is the highest of Barcelona's hills, and on smog-free days the entire city is laid out spectacularly before you. Indeed, so splendid is the sight that it gave rise to Tibidabo's name, which is from the Latin for "I shall give to you"— the words used by the Devil to tempt Christ. But the first thing you see as you get out of the funicular is the enormous Basilica (Temple Expiatori del Sagrat Cor), completed in 1960. There's a lift up to the roof, from where marvellous views extend out to the sea and inland over the forested north side of the mountain. Next to the funicular is the entrance to the **funfair**. This has various rides and attractions, including a ferris wheel and a roller coaster. • Park: Summer Wed–Sun noon–9, 10 or 11pm; restricted hours at other times; check www.tibidabo.cat for details ☎ 93 211 79 42 🚋 to Av. Tibidabo, then Tramvia Blau and funicular. Alternatively there is also the T2A bus from Plaça Catalunya (in front of the Caja Madrid Bank), leaving from 10.15 onwards on the days the funpark is open.

Torre de Collserola (map 3) Norman Foster's 288-m-high telecommunications tower was built so that the 1992 Olympics could be beamed around the world. You can take an external glass lift 115 m up to the observation deck, where the view extends for 70 km. • Same opening days as Tibidabo (above) but with shorter hours ☎ 93 211 79 42 🚋 to Av. Tibidabo, then Tramvia Blau and funicular. Alternatively there is also the T2A bus from Plaça Catalunya (in front of the Caja Madrid Bank), leaving from 10.15 onwards on the days the funpark is open.

CosmoCaixa (map 3) This exciting science museum at the foot of Tibidabo is set in a daring underground edifice, with plenty of open space and parkland overhead. The main scientific principles are presented through interactive exhibits and multimedia displays that make science fun for all ages. Highlights include the Geography Wall showing massive rock types and a gigantic Foucault's Pendulum. The Sunken Forest is a reconstructed slice of the Amazon jungle, animals and all. It's great for kids; take a picnic and make a day of it. • Tues–Sun 10am–8pm ☎ 93 212 60 50 • C/Isaac Newton 26 🚋 to Avinguda Tibidabo then 10-minute walk

Monestir de Pedralbes (map 3) The monastery was founded in 1326 by Queen Elisenda, wife of Jaume II, and still houses a community of nuns. Immediately after the entrance is the beautiful, three-storey colonnaded cloister, one of the jewels of Catalan Gothic architecture. Just to the right, the Capella de Sant Miquel is covered with frescoes dating from 1346, by the Catalan artist Ferrer Bassa. You'll also find around the cloister a medieval pharmacy, the 15th-century refectory and kitchen, a Renaissance hospital and, back at the entrance, the Chapter House of 1419. • April–end Sept Tues–Sun 10am–5pm; Sat 10am–7pm; Sun 10am–8pm; rest of the year Tue–Fri 10am–2pm, Sat–Sun 10am–5pm ☎ 93 256 34 34 • Baixada del Monestir 9 🚇 to Reina Elisenda and 10 min walk

Colònia Güell (map 3) In the attempt to quell worker unrest in Barcelona, some of the wealthy elite sponsored industrial colonies away from the city. These were designed to be Catholic and conservative communities, where the owner would provide a miniature welfare state for his workers and in return the workers would, it was hoped, refrain from industrial disputes. The Colònia Güell was another of Eusebi Güell's grand schemes, and this cloth-making colony out in the village of Santa Coloma eventually failed. But Gaudí left his mark on the place. He designed the church for the colony, and began work in 1899, but only the crypt was completed. Set on a pine-covered hill, it is typically surreal, and mysteriously organic. There are no external buttresses or supports. The huge columns and ceiling are held up in a perfectly calculated tension, like a cat's cradle raised to the level of architectural form. • Mon–Fri 10am–7pm (5pm Nov–April), Saturday and Sunday 10am–3pm ☎ 93 630 58 07 • C/Claudi Güell s/n 🚇 Colonia Güell

Museu Blau (off map after H5) This new museum is situated in the Edifici Fòrum—a stunning showpiece building by the Swiss architects Herzog & de Meuron, built for the 2004 Universal Forum of Cultures. The museum is now a cultural icon for Barcelona. In contrast to its cutting edge home, the exhibits date back centuries, fruit of the city's Natural Sciences collections. Fossils, stuffed animals, and rock and plant specimens relate the gradual evolution of the earth. • Tue–Sat 10am–7pm, Sun and bank holidays 10am–8pm ☎ 93 256 60 02 • Plaça Leonardo da Vinci (Parc del Fòrum) ⬧ El Maresme – Fòrum

WALKING TOUR: AROUND BARCELONA

Be sure to wear a sturdy pair of walking shoes for this extensive tour of Barcelona's fascinating outer districts. The **Parc Joan Miró** is opposite the Tarragona metro station. Laid out on the site of a former slaughterhouse, it contains Miró's iconic 22-m-high sculpture of a woman and bird, *Dona i Ocell*.

Head up C/de Tarragona and turn left at **Plaça dels Països Catalans**—a radically Modernist square that caused considerable controversy when it was laid out in 1983—to reach the entrance of the **Parc de l'Espanya Industrial**. This is an intriguing mix of pleasure-park and post-industrial art-work, with a cast-iron sculptural dragon that's also a children's slide and a boating lake overlooked by ten towers.

From Plaça de Joan Peiró on the opposite side of the park, walk up the C/del Vallespir, leading through the heart of Sants, a pretty neighbourhood with many bars and cafés. Turn left at Travessera de les Corts. After around 600 m you'll arrive at the burning cauldron of Catalonian pride, otherwise known as **Camp Nou**, the home ground of Barcelona FC. Just before the stadium, C/de la Maternitat leads towards Plaça de Pius XII on Avinguda Diagonal. Turn left here, and on the right you will see the Italian Renaissance-style **Palau Reial de Pedralbes**, built in 1919 for Gaudí's patron Count Eusebi Güell. If you want to stay outdoors before moving on, take a look at the Palau's superb gardens, where there's a fountain designed by Gaudí.

Around the corner, on Avinguda de Pedralbes, look out for the extraordinary iron dragon guarding the gate of the **Finca Güell**, one of Gaudí's earliest works. At the top end of this street, the beautiful **Monestir de Pedralbes** is a supreme example of Catalan Gothic architecture. It's worth pausing here to admire the church's artworks and to take a stroll around the delightful 14th-century three-storey cloister. To the rear of the monastery, is the **Església de Pedralbes** where the original order of nuns worship and sing vespers.

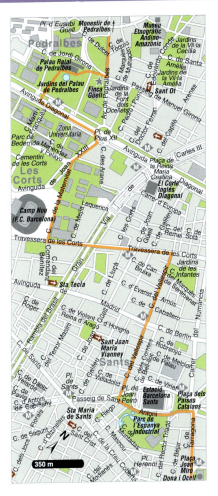

Here be dragons! A varied but long walk outside the city centre.

Start:
Parc Joan Miró
◈ Tarragona, Espanya

Finish:
Monestir de Pedralbes
☷ Reina Elisenda

RETAIL THERAPY

Like any other major European city, Barcelona has its fair share of large department stores and shopping centres, along with international chain stores and familiar high-street retail outlets, most of which can be found around Avinguda del Portal de l'Àngel and Carrer Portaferrissa at the Plaça de Catalunya end of La Rambla. But its real shopping strong points are in more specialized areas where local—and ultra-stylish—talents come into their own, such as fashion and jewellery, interior design and household goods, art and antiques, and, of course, food and drink.

The Ciutat Vella is still the place to look for antiques, antiquarian books and fine art—though at a price. Many of the city's top art salesrooms are in and around C/Petrixol in the Barri Gòtic (Gothic Quarter). Catalan ceramics range from the primitive to the most sophisticated; specialist shops are scattered across the city, including a few half-hidden in the narrow streets around the cathedral.

Jewellery, handmade rustic furniture, hand-knitted items and other high-quality craft goods, as well as some of the artisans themselves, may be found at the Poble Espanyol in Montjuïc and the streets around the Picasso Museum in C/Montcada.

Textile making has a long history in Catalonia. It was the principal industry during the industrial revolution, but it is only in recent years that local fashion designers have started to make an international name for themselves; most notably Javier Simorra, Lydia Delgado—a former ballerina—and Custo (born as Ángel Custodio Dalmau Salmons), whose funky, hand-printed T-shirts have become coveted items both here and abroad. Look for their creations in shops along the boulevards and in the arcades and galleries of the Eixample district along the Avinguda Diagonal, where you will also find the big name boutiques.

Lovers of luxury leather goods should not miss Loewe's beautiful Modernista showcase on Passeig de Gràcia. The tiny streets near the Mercat del Born in La Ribera are Barcelona's answer to London's Covent Garden, with small shops selling modern, local fashions and design. Fashionistas are already shifting their attention to El Raval (near the MACBA) and Gràcia (particularly along the C/d'Astúries)—the city's latest fashion hubs.

Department stores and shopping centres

If you are short of time, Barcelona has some excellent one-stop shopping venues that are never second best for quality and style. The venerable **El Corte Inglés**, Plaça de Catalunya 14, is a Barcelona landmark, selling cosmetics, clothes, household goods and fine food and drink. One of its several branches can be found at Avinguda del Portal de l'Àngel 19 which specializes in sports wear and equipment, music and young fashion.

In the Zona Alta, **L'Illa Diagonal**, Avinguda Diagonal 557 is an upmarket shopping centre with a good selection of clothes, shoes, accessories and gifts, as well as gourmet food and wine shops in the basement.

Close to the centre, in the Port Vell, **Maremagnum**, which is reached by crossing the drawbridge in front of the Columbus Monument, has around 30 shops, from Xocoa chocolates to H&M, and is open seven days a week.

Designer fashion & furnishings

Agatha Ruiz de la Prada is famous for her bright, block-coloured creations for women's and children's wear (C/Consell de Cent 314–316). If you are looking for high-end fashion, then you will be spoiled for choice at the Eixample: here too, are **Armand Basi**, Passeig de Gràcia 49, and **Purificación García**, C/de Provença 292, all of which will allow you to leave Barcelona looking dressed to kill. But for pure trendiness, it has to be a T-shirt from **Custo Barcelona**, which has three outlets in town; one of

flickr.com/Belvisto, –/Purplevovet, –/Ramirez

them is situated in Plaça de les Olles 7, in the Born district. And of course you will find several **Desigual** stores scattered around the city.

With its great Modernista history, Barcelona is also a centre for the best in interior design, and nowhere does it better than **Vinçon**, Passeig de Gràcia 96, with ultra-contemporary furniture, kitchenware, bathroom accessories and a myriad of other stylish objects you didn't realise you needed—or wanted—so much.

Just off La Rambla, stop at **Art Escudellers**, C/dels Escudellers 23, for ceramics, tiles, glassware, costume jewellery and all sorts of crafts by Spanish designers.

Alida

Art and antiques

The **Bulevard dels Antiquaris** at Passeig de Gràcia 55 contains around 70 antique shops, enough to keep the most avid collector happy. Commercial art galleries are clustered along the C/Portixol in the Barri Gòtic and near the Picasso Museum on C/Montcada in the Born. For underground and graffiti art, check out **Base Elements** in the Barri Gótic (C/del Palau 6). If you are brave and have stellar bargaining powers, **Els Encants Vells**—the centuries old flea market that has recently been given a stunning new home near Plaça de les Glòries Catalanes—can throw up the odd piece of treasure.

Food and drink

The magnificent **Mercat de la Boqueria** on La Rambla will cater to most culinary requirements. But for more specialized fare head to **Formatgeria La Seu**, C/Dagueria 16, which sells fabulous artisan cheeses from all over Spain; **Casa Gispert**, C/Sombrerers 23, with the best home-roasted nuts in town; **Pasteleria Escribà**, La Rambla 83, a chocoholic's heaven; **Caelum** near the cathedral at C/de la Palla 8 for sweets, honey, jam, olives and other produce from monastery kitchens, and **Vila Viniteca**, C/Agullers 7, with a choice of thousands of different Catalan and Spanish wines.

commons.wikimedia.org

EXCURSIONS

There's an amazing diversity of things to see and do in such a pocket-sized region—you can hike in the High Pyrenees, bask on a Costa Brava beach, go wine-tasting in ancient vineyards and yet never be more than 150 km from Barcelona. The places recommended here are popular day trips from the city, and most can easily be reached by train or bus.

THE REGION AT A GLANCE

Girona (map 4) Northern Catalonia's largest city was founded by the Romans, for whom the location on a hill by the River Onyar made it perfect as a means of protecting the route from France to the south. Throughout the early part of its history it was at least as important as Barcelona, and the medieval walled city that you can see today contains some fine buildings from that period. The **cathedral** stands at the top of a huge flight of 91 steps leading up from the Plaça de la Catedral. The church was begun in the 13th century and contains a vast Gothic nave (one of the largest in the world). Look out too for the fine Romanesque cloister, adorned with sculptures representing figures of the Old Testament. In the Treasury, see the splendid Tapestry of the Creation, in its own room. Head down the steps again to reach the **church of Sant Feliu**. Its distinctive truncated tower is the result of a strike by lightning in 1581. The church itself marries Romanesque, Gothic and baroque styles. Nearby are the **Banys Àrabs**, Arab baths that are still in operation. They date from the 12th century, and so were in fact built long after the Arab occupation of the city. The architect was certainly influenced by Moorish design, however, and the baths stand as an unusual

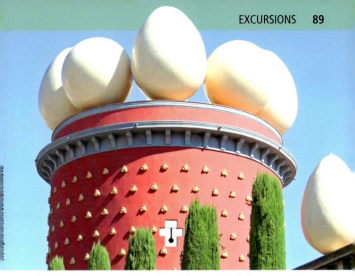

Dalí built his museum on the ruins of the municipal theatre at Figueres, destroyed at the end of the Spanish Civil War.

Moorish-Romanesque hybrid. Leading south from Plaça de la Catedral, the Carrer de la Força runs through the **Call**, Girona's medieval Jewish district. You can get a flavour of how it once was at the **Museu d'Història dels Jueus**, a maze of rooms and stairways around an inner courtyard that stood at the centre of the Call. For an overview of Girona, climb to the **Passeig Arqueològic**, from where you can walk along the ancient walls and look out across the rooftops and church spires of the city. 🚆 from Barcelona-Sants and Passeig de Gràcia stations

Figueres (map 4) This small town acts as a hub for the northern part of the Costa Brava. It has a bustling Rambla, the 18th century Castell de Sant Ferran, last stronghold of the Republicans at the end of the Spanish Civil War, and the Museu de l'Empordà, with Greek and Roman archaeological finds and a collection of Catalan art. But it would rarely rate a mention if it weren't for the birth here in 1904 of the great Surrealist painter and all-round eccentric, Salvador Dalí. The **Teatre-Museu Dalí** was designed by the artist as a monument to his own fantastic vision of the world, something evident in every part of the museum, from the giant Dalíesque eggs on the outer walls to the bizarre installations inside. The paintings on display are drawn from all periods of Dalí's life, and include such typically unnerving challenges to normality as *The Spectre of Sex Appeal* and *Self-portrait with Fried Bacon*. In the Sala de Mae West, an entire room is designed as a grand portrait to the Hollywood actress, with the sofa as her lips, fireplaces as her nostrils and so on. Dalí died in Figueres in 1989, and as a final touch of the macabre was buried in his own museum. **Teatre–Museu Dalí: Plaça Gala–Salvador Dalí 5. In general Tue–Sun (and Mondays October–March 1), 9.30–6pm; Nov 1–end Feb 10.30 am, March 1–end June and October 9.30am–6pm, July–end Sept 9am–8pm. Last entry 45 min before closing.** ☎ 972 67 75 00 ➹ from Barcelona-Sants and Passeig de Gràcia stations

Montserrat (map 3) Montserrat lies 40 km northwest of Barcelona. Its name, "serrated mountain", perfectly describes its appearance, a 1,200-m-high mass of jagged rock. In the 9th century, legend has it, the lost statue of the Black Virgin brought to Spain by St Peter was discovered here. Miraculously unable to be removed from the mountain, it was kept in place and a Benedictine monastery built around it instead. Perched dramatically on the side of the mountain and reached by a stunning cable-car ride, the current **Basilica** dates from the 16th century, though it was severely damaged by Napoleon's troops in 1813 and had to be substantially rebuilt. Montserrat is today one of Spain's pre-eminent pilgrimage sites and stands at the spiritual heart of Catalonia—its religious importance meant it was always able to retain its independence from Madrid, and the monks maintained Catalan as a language of learning even during the years of Franco's ban. The statue of the Black Virgin is above the high altar of the basilica. If possible, you should also try to attend the **Salve Regina** (see below for times) or the Vespers daily at 6.45pm. which are sung by the famous Montserrat Boys' Choir, the oldest in Europe. In one of the monastery buildings nearby is the **Museu de Montserrat**, with an interesting collection that contains archaeological finds, religious artefacts and paintings and sculptures by El Greco, Caravaggio, Picasso, Dalí and several Catalan artists. Best of all, perhaps, are the scenic walks which you can take from the monastery. You can also ascend higher up the mountain via a funicular to the **Sant Joan** hermitage. A brisk one-hour walk from here brings you to **Sant Jeroni** near the peak, where the views of

Montserrat's great saw-tooth pinnacles are spectacular. • Basilica open daily 7.30am–8pm (Viewings of the 'Black Virgin' 8–10.30pm, noon–6.30pm). Mass with choir: Mon–Fri 1pm, Sun noon. • Museu de Montserrat daily 10am–5.30pm ☎ (Tourist Office) 93 877 77 77 ✉ from Espanya to Aeri de Montserrat (line 5), then cable car or funicolar (cremallera)

Penedès (map 5) Catalonia's most productive wine region is the Penedès, a mere 50 km west of Barcelona. This is where some of the country's best red and white wines hail from, and it's also the home of *cava*, Spain's version of champagne. If you want to tour the vineyards, you'll probably be best off going by car. The area's main town is **Vilafranca del Penedès**, where you can gain some preliminary knowledge of Catalan winemaking at the enjoyable **VINSEUM–Museu de les Cultures del Vi** (Plaça Jaume I 5). The town holds a wine festival each autumn to celebrate the grape harvest—the main events take place on the first Sunday in October. A few kilometres to the northwest, **Bodegas Torres** is the region's leading producer. If it's *cava* you crave, head for nearby **Sant Sadurní d'Anoia**. The vineyards around here turn out almost all of the country's entire output. Just outside town, the **Caves Codorníu** vineyard is worth heading for, and not just for its wine. The main building is a Modernista work designed by Puig i Cadafalch in the late 19th century. • VINSEUM ☎ 93 890 05 82 • Bodegas Torres: tours Mon–Sat 9.15am–4.45pm, Sun 9.15am–1pm (book through www.torres.es) • Caves Codorníu: tours Mon–Fri 9am–5pm; Sat, Sun to 1pm ☎ 93 891 33 42 or book through reserves@codorniu.es • For more details on individual vineyards and visiting times (booking essential), call the tourist office in Vilafranca del Penedès, ☎ 93 818 12 54, C/Cort 14 ➡ from Barcelona-Sants or Plaça Catalunya stations to Sant Sadurní d'Anoia and Vilafranca del Penedès

Sitges (map 5) Sitges is 40 km south of Barcelona on the Costa Daurada and one of Spain's liveliest Mediterranean resorts, with a famously high-energy nightlife. The town first came to the world's attention in the 1890s, when the Modernista painter Santiago Rusiñol set up a studio here that attracted followers from Barcelona's art set. Sitges's second wave of popularity started in the 1960s when it gained its current reputation as a hedonistic party town. It's popular with a wide range of people, from trendy Barceloneses to holidaying families as well as being one of the biggest gay destinations in Europe. By day, the action centres on the resort's string of nine sandy beaches. You can take in the scene whilst walking along the **Passeig Marítim**. If the beach culture gets too hot to handle, head for the town. The city end of the promenade leads to the 17th-century baroque church of **Sant Bartomeu i Santa Tecla**, with a street of beautiful old whitewashed houses nearby. One hosts the **Museu Cau Ferrat**, in Rusiñol's former studio, another, the **Museu Maricel**, whilst the new **Casa Bacardí** (Plaça Ajuntament 11) has a permanent display on one of Sitges's most famous emigres. Contemporary art has a place in Sitges too. The **Fundació Stämpfli** exposes works from artists of the ilk of Joel Peter Witkin and Eduardo Arroyo. • Fundació Stämpfli (C/d'en Bosc): July–Sept Tues–Sat 10am–2pm and 4pm–8pm, Sun 10am–3pm; rest of the year, Tues–Fri 3.30pm–7pm, Sat 10am–2pm and 3.30pm–7pm, Sun 11am–3pm. Tourist Office (Plaça Eduard Maristany 2) ☎ 93 894 42 51 ⊠ from Barcelona-Sants and Passeig de Gràcia stations.

Upper courtyard of the Museu Maricel at Sitges.

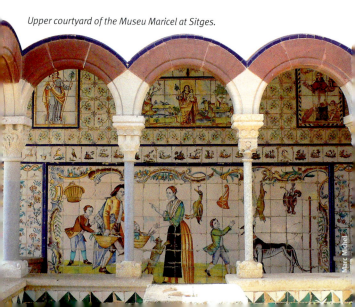

Marc Michel

Tarragona (map 5) The hilltop town of Tarragona was founded by the Romans in the 3rd century BC, and it was their principal city in this part of Spain. As such, it has a far greater collection of Roman remains than Barcelona. Down towards the sea is the **Amfiteatre**, once the site of gladiatorial combat. Roman sports fans would also be found at the **Circ Romà**, whose ruins are just above the amphitheatre, and which was where chariot races took place. At the southern end of the old town, the **Museu Nacional Arqueològic** has a vast collection of Roman finds, including a magnificent group of mosaics. The ticket also gives admission to the **Necropolis**, to the west of town. At the centre of Tarragona is a splendid tangle of medieval streets, many of whose houses are partly constructed from earlier Roman stonework. They lead to the great 12th–13th century **Catedral**, whose façade demonstrates an effortless transition from Romanesque to Gothic. From the cathedral, work your way round to the **Passeig Arqueològic**, which gives fantastic views of the sea and the city and runs between the original Roman walls and those erected by the British during the War of the Spanish Succession 2,000 years later. Tarragona, the capital of the Costa Daurada, also has some fine beaches as its doorstep. One of the prettiest is **Altafulla**, which boasts a unique string of fishermen's shacks known as the *botigues del mar* and an impressive medieval castle. Nerby, you can combine bird watching and sunbathing at **Tamarit beach**, which borders on a nature reserve • Tarragona Tourist Office (C/Major 39) ☎ 97 725 07 95 • Altafulla Tourist Office (Plaça del Pou 1) ☎ 97 765 14 26 🚆 from Barcelona-Estació França, Sants and Passeig de Gràcia stations

PortAventura (map 5) Near the resort of Salou, this theme park offers some of the most exciting rides in the world, including the infamous Dragon Khan, and Furius Baco, the fastest roller-coaster in Europe. The park Its activities combine cultural information and cutting-edge technology. It is divided into "villages" representing the American Far West, Polynesia, China, Mediterrania and Mexico, all with their themed rides, shows and restaurants. The highlights, apart from the roller coasters, are shooting the rapids in the Far West, exploring underwater in Polynesia's Sea Odyssey, marvelling at the Maya ruins in Mexico, and chilling out in a Mediterranean fishing village with a typical seafood meal. Queues can be extremely long in summer, in which case try **PortAventura Aquatic Park** at the same location. ☎ 902 20 22 20; www.portaventura.es 🚆 from Barcelona-Estació Francia, Sants and Passeig de Gràcia stations

cityBites

Compared with other major European cities, restaurants are good value in Barcelona, and you can usually eat as well at a small local taverna as at a fancy hotel. At lunchtime, be sure to check out the *menú del día*, two or three courses plus wine and bread which most restaurants offer at a surprisingly low price. The following recommendations are categorized to give some idea of what you might expect to pay per head for a three-course evening meal excluding drinks:

1 = budget price
2 = 30–40 euros
3 = over 40 euros

◀ *Barcelona is one of the best dining destinations in Europe.*

Bar Lobo

LA RAMBLA AND CUITAT VELLA

Bar Lobo
✧ Catalunya or Liceu
C/Pintor Fortuny 3
☎ 93 481 53 46
Sun–Wed 9am–midnight
Thurs–Sat 9am–2.30am
[1]

Friendly and refined, not far from La Rambla dels Estudis. It serves excellent tapas, either in a colourful indoor setting or on an outdoor terrace.

Bun Bo
✧ Jaume I
C/Sagristans 3
☎ 93 301 13 78
Open 1pm–midnight
(1am Fri, Sat)
[1]

For a change of pace to tapas and tortillas, this Vietnamese eatery close to the cathedral offers quick and tasty noodle dishes and soups. Outdoor terrace in summer, colourful oriental decor within.

Cafè de L'Acadèmia
✧ Jaume I
C/Lledó 1
☎ 93 315 00 26
Mon–Fri 1.30–4pm and 8.30–11.30pm
[2]

With its postcard location it may look expensive, but this restaurant of contemporary Catalan market cuisine is one of the remaining value-for-money places in the Barri Gòtic. In the summer, go for one of the candle-lit outdoor table. Bookings essential.

Cal Pep
✧ Jaume I
Plaça de les Olles 8
☎ 93 310 79 61
Mon 7.30–11.30pm,
Tues–Fri 1–3.45pm and 7.30–11.30pm, Sat 1–3.45pm
[2]–[3]

For many connoisseurs, this tiny tapas bar serves the best seafood in Barcelona. Get there early to score a seat at the bar and watch the maestro grill chefs go to work.

Can Culleretes
✧ Liceu
C/Quintana 5
☎ 93 317 64 85
Tues–Sat 1.30–4pm,
9–11pm, Sun 1.30–4pm;
closed July
[2]

Barcelona's oldest restaurant was founded in 1786 and serves time-honoured traditional Catalan cuisine.

Comerç 24
✧ Jaume I
C/Comerç 24
☎ 93 319 21 02
Tues–Sat 1.30–3.30pm, 8.30pm–11pm,
Reservations required
[3]

Find out the buzz on Catalonia's new wave of cooking at this stylish eatery where combinations and presentation defy imagination.

Cuines Santa Caterina
✧ Jaume I
Francesc Cambó 16

Els Quatre Gats menu

flickr.com/Lance And Erin

☎ 93 268 99 18
Sun–Wed 1–4pm and
8–11.30pm, Thurs–Sat
1–4pm and
8pm–00.30am. No
reservations.
1

This stylish, canteen-style
eatery is located inside
the Santa Caterina
covered market, handy for
sourcing the freshest
ingredients for their
excellent cuisine. From
sushi to salad and pasta,
it's all here. Tables come
on a first served basis so
it's worth getting
there a few minutes
before opening times,
especially on the
weekends.

Els Quatre Gats

◆ Catalunya,
Urquinaona
C/Montsió 3bis
☎ 93 302 41 40
Restaurant daily
1pm–1am
Bar daily 10am–1am
2 – 3

A Modernista landmark:
the building is by Puig i
Cadafalch, the
restaurant was once
frequented by artists such
as Ramon Casas and
Rusiñol; the menu cover
was designed by none
other than Picasso. Bar-
café at the front, good
Catalan restaurant at the
back.

Ocaña

◆ Liceu, Drassanes
Plaça Reial 13–15
☎ 93 676 48 14
Mon–Thurs
5pm–2.30am, Sat
11am–3pm and Sun
11am–5pm
1

This spectacular bar and
bistro, right on the
Plaça Reial, drips in the
faded glory that this part
of the old city is famous
for. Light, creative dishes
can be enjoyed in various,
eclectic dining rooms, or
on the outdoor
terrace, watching the
animated street life on
the square.

Pla

◆ Liceu, Jaume I
C/Bellafila 5
☎ 93 412 65 52
Sun–Thurs
7.30pm–midnight, Fri
and Sat 7pm–00.30am
2

East meets West in this
modern restaurant mixing
local, Middle Eastern and
Asian cuisines in smart
surroundings. There is
another branch (called
Bar de Pla) at
C/Montcada 2
specializing in *tapas*.

Senyor Parellada

◆ Jaume I
C/ Argenteria 37
☎ 93 310 50 94

Daily 1–3.45µ
8.30–11.30pr
2

A perennially f
bistro that serves up
excellent Catalan market
cuisine and has a great
wine list. Try the *botifarra*
sausage and grilled
sardines.

Taller de Tapas

◆ Liceu
Plaça Sant Josep Oriol 9
☎ 93 301 80 20
Mon–Sat 8.30am–1am,
Sun noon–1am
2

A good initiation to the
tapeo, this restaurant
boasts an extensive menu
of delectable morsels that
come flying out of their
gleaming open kitchen.
Four other branches in
Barcelona; visit
www.tallerdetapas.com.

EL RAVAL

Bar Moritz

◆ Universitat or
Sant Antoni
Ronda de Sant Antoni 41
☎ 93 426 00 50
Daily 6am–3am
1 – 3

Moritz beer is to
Barcelona what Carlsberg
is to Copenhagen. On the
edge of the Raval, the
brand's old brewery has
been stunningly
transformed by the French

designer Jean Nouvel. There's something for most tastes; an excellent tapas bar, a bistro, and a shop selling beer, wine, bread and magazines.

Casa Leopoldo
◈ Sant Antoni
C/Sant Rafael 24
☎ 93 441 30 14
Tues–Fri
1.30pm–3.30pm,
8.30pm–11pm; Sat,
1.30pm–4pm and
8.30pm–11pm and Sun
1.30pm–4pm
③

This elegant, neighbourhood favourite has been going strong since 1929 and its tile and white tablecloth decor seems to have changed little since then. Dishes to order include sticky pork with apple and pine nuts relish and scrambled eggs with wild mushrooms. Classy midday menu for €25.

Granja M. Viader
◈ Liceu
C/d'En Xúcla 4–6
☎ 93 318 34 86
Mon–Sat 9am–1.15 and
5pm–9.15
①

A *granja* is a café that specialises in milk-based drinks and other dairy products, and this is one of the most famous. Step

inside the traditional, tiled interior for a hot chocolate, *café con leche* or *cacaolat* (chocolate milk).

Las Fernández
◈ Liceu or Paral.lel
C/ de les Carretes 11
☎ 93 443 20 43
Tues–Thurs and Sun
9pm–2am, Fri and Sat
9pm–3am
②

This popular eatery serves up great local market cuisine with a few Brazilian touches thrown into the eclectic mix. The atmosphere is lively and you may have to wait outside in the street to be seated. However, the hosts are always friendly and accommodating.

La Verònica
◈ Liceu
Rambla del Raval 2–4
☎ 93 329 33 03
Daily 1pm–Midnight
(1am on Thurs, Fri, Sat)
①

The popularity of this pizza joint never seems to waiver. Wafer-thin pizza bases are topped with excellent local ingredients such as *botifarra* sausage and jamón iberico. It's perpetually buzzing with hip locals, who cram into the minimalist, sleek decor.

Tara Stevens

Agua

Mesón David
◈ Paral.lel
C/de les Carretes 63
☎ 93 441 59 34
Daily noon–4pm,
8pm–midnight
②

Tucked away in the Barri Xino, this restaurant has tasty, hearty dishes from all over Spain, served with a smile and a sense of fun.

WATERFRONT

Agua
◈ Ciutadella–Vila Olímpica
Pg. Marítim de la Barceloneta 30
☎ 93 225 12 72
Daily 1–3.45pm (Sat, Sun 4.30pm) and
8–11.30pm (Fri, Sat 00.30am)
②

One of your best bets in the touristy Olympic Village area. An upmarket, split-level restaurant that offers a beautiful view and innovative fish dishes.

Bestial
✧ Ciutadella–Vila Olímpica
C/Ramón
Trias Fargas 2–4
☎ 93 224 04 07
Daily 1–4pm (Sat, Sun 4.30pm); Sun–Thurs 8pm–11.30pm; Fri and Sat 8pm–midnight
1 – 2

Dine beneath the fins of Frank Gehry's famous fish sculpture in this al fresco eatery that serves delicious, light Mediterranean cuisine.

Els Pescadors
✧ Poblenou
Plaça Prim 1
☎ 93 225 20 18
Daily 1–3.45pm and 8–11.30; closed Dec 21–Jan 2
3

Located on a delightful square in the old fishing village of Poblenou. Marvellously fresh fish is cooked in the best modern Catalan style.

Pez Vela
✧ Barceloneta
Passeig del Mare

Nostrum 19–21
☎ 93 221 63 17
Daily 1–4pm and 8–11pm (midnight on Fri, Sat)
2

Situated at the base of the landmark W Hotel, Pez Vela excels in fresh seafood dishes and delicious paella. Its smart, casual surroundings include an outdoor terrace, facing the beach.

7 Portes
✧ Barceloneta
Passeig Isabel II 14
☎ 93 319 30 33
Open daily 1pm–1am
3

Stylish restaurant that has remained largely unchanged since its foundation in 1836. An extensive menu of Catalan specialities and a hunger-busting range of

Bestial

paellas. A great favourite, so booking is advisable for evenings.

Torre d'Alta Mar
✧ Barceloneta
Pg. Joan de Borbó 88
☎ 93 221 00 07
Sun, Mon 8–11.30pm
Tues–Sat 1–3.30pm and 8–11.30pm
3

Treat yourself to the ultimate blowout by booking a table at this swish restaurant perched at 75 m on top of the Torre de Sant Sebastiá cable car tower. The cuisine is as spectacular as the 360-degree view.

POBLE SEC AND MONTJUÏC

Cañota – Casa de Tapas
✧ Espanya
C/ Llerida 7
☎ 93 325 91 71
Tues–Sat 1pm–4 pm and 7.30pm–Midnight, Sun, 1pm–4pm
1

Part of the growing restaurant scene near the Plaça España, Cañota is a fun place to try all manner of tapas. Colourful decor, space and good table service combine to provide a children-friendly environment. Ideal for your first tapas foray.

Federal
⌖ Poble Sec or Sant Antoni
C/Parlament 39
☎ 93 187 36 07
Mon–Thurs 8am–11pm, Fri 8am–1am, Sat 9am–1am, Sun 9am–5.30pm
1 – 2

With long, pinewood tables and Scandinavian design, Federal Café wouldn't look out of place in Sweden or Sydney. Barceloneses flock here on the weekends for an excellent brunch. All ingredients are organic.

La Bella Napoli
⌖ Paral.lel
C/Margarit 12
☎ 93 442 50 56
Daily 1.30–4pm and 8.30pm–midnight
1

It's loud, frantically busy and for its fans does the best pizzas in town. Jovial Italian waiters also serve pasta and salad dishes.

Quimet & Quimet
⌖ Paral.lel
C/Poeta Cabanyes 25
☎ 93 442 31 42
Mon–Fri noon–4pm and 7–10.30pm, Sat noon–4pm
2

This tiny, traditional hole-in-the-wall has a fan club stretching the globe.

Tara Stevens

Quimet & Quimet

The *montaditos* (a Spanish version of *canapés*) are superb, as is the selection of local wines. The fact that it has standing room only adds to the unique experience.

EIXAMPLE AND GRÀCIA

Alta Taberna Paco Meralgo
⌖ Hospital Clínic
C/Muntaner 171
☎ 93 430 90 27
Daily 1–4pm and 8pm–00.30am
2 – 3

High quality *tapas* and "half portions" have made this new restaurant a runaway success. The decor is smoothly stylish and upmarket, as is the clientele, which includes the odd celebrity.

Bilbao
⌖ Fontana, Diagonal
C/Perill 33
☎ 93 458 96 24
Mon–Sat 1–4pm and 9–11pm
2 – 3

Top-notch, traditional Basque cuisine is served in this evergreen, florid tile restaurant that is enormously popular with locals.

Botafumeiro
⌖ Fontana
C/Gran de Gràcia 81
☎ 93 218 42 30
Open daily Noon–1am
3

Treat yourself to what is generally agreed to be the best upmarket shellfish in Barcelona.

Can Ravell
⌖ Girona
C/Aragó 313
☎ 93 457 51 14
Tues–Sat 10am–7pm, Sun 10am–1pm
2 – 3

One of the city's most authentic and appreciated dining experiences, Can Ravell is a traditional *colmado* (deli/grocery shop) with a minuscule dining room up a flight of rickety stairs. Dishes change almost daily and are made using the freshest possible ingredients, lovingly prepared.

El Glop
✧ Fontana, Joanic
C/Sant Lluís 24
☎ 93 213 70 58
Daily 1–4pm, 8pm–1am
① – ②
Fast-paced and ever-popular, this enjoyable taverna specializes in char-grilled meats, and is also a good place for *torrades*, the toasted version of *pa amb tomàquet*.

Mordisco
✧ Diagonal
Passatge de la Concepció 10
☎ 93 487 96 56
Daily 12.30pm–00.30am, Thurs–Sat 12.30pm–2am
③
Contemporary, market fresh Catalan and Spanish dishes are severed in a delightful, light-filled space spread over two storeys. For lunch, take a table in the winter garden, whilst post-dinner you can retire to the cosy first floor lounge.

Roca Moo and Roca Bar
✧ Diagonal
C/Roselló 265
☎ 93 445 40 00
Roca Moo: Tues–Sat 1.30–4pm and 8.30–11pm. Roca Bar: 1pm–1am
③
Located inside the fashionable Hotel Omm, the Roca brothers, who have a famed restaurant in Girona, treat you to their culinary magic. Roca Moo is a formal affair whilst the adjacent Roca Bar lets you sample inventive dishes in a relaxed setting.

Tragaluz
✧ Diagonal
Passatge de la Concepció 5
☎ 93 487 06 21
Daily 1.30–4pm and 8.30pm–11.30pm
③
Founded back in the 1980s, the restaurant was something of a groundbreaker in terms of design and style of food, which rendered traditional dishes with a modern twist. It's just been renovated (an oyster bar is now part of the deal) yet the menu is as superb as ever.

AROUND BARCELONA

ABaC
🖉 Tibidabo
Avda Tibidabo 1
☎ 93 319 66 00
Tues–Sat 1.30–4pm, 8.30–11pm
③
This haute cuisine restaurant has a superb setting in a high-design mansion at the base of Tibidabo. The young chef Jordi Cruz has rightly earnt two Michelin stars for his imaginative cuisine served in a simple yet elegant dining room with an adjacent garden.

Can Travi Nou
✧ Horta
C/Jorge Manrique 8
☎ 93 428 03 01
Mon–Sat 1.30–4pm and 8.30–11pm; Sun 1.30–4pm
③
Traditional Catalan dishes served in a beautifully conserved *masia* (farmhouse). Outside tables available.

El Asador de Aranda
🖉 Tibidabo
Av. Tibidabo 31
☎ 93 417 01 15
Mon–Sat 1.30–4pm, 8–11pm; Sun 1.30–4pm
③
This is the most spectacular branch of the famed Castilian carvery. Be prepared to gorge on succulent meats in an elegant Modernista mansion.

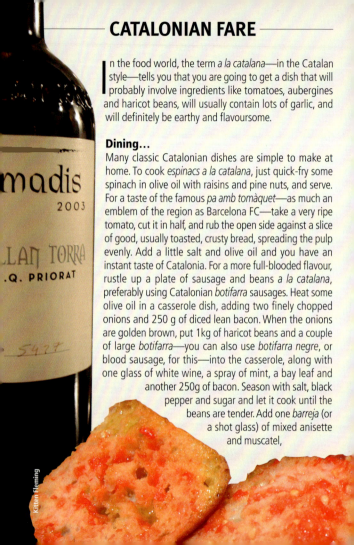

CATALONIAN FARE

In the food world, the term *a la catalana*—in the Catalan style—tells you that you are going to get a dish that will probably involve ingredients like tomatoes, aubergines and haricot beans, will usually contain lots of garlic, and will definitely be earthy and flavoursome.

Dining…

Many classic Catalonian dishes are simple to make at home. To cook *espinacs a la catalana*, just quick-fry some spinach in olive oil with raisins and pine nuts, and serve. For a taste of the famous *pa amb tomàquet*—as much an emblem of the region as Barcelona FC—take a very ripe tomato, cut it in half, and rub the open side against a slice of good, usually toasted, crusty bread, spreading the pulp evenly. Add a little salt and olive oil and you have an instant taste of Catalonia. For a more full-blooded flavour, rustle up a plate of sausage and beans *a la catalana*, preferably using Catalonian *botifarra* sausages. Heat some olive oil in a casserole dish, adding two finely chopped onions and 250 g of diced lean bacon. When the onions are golden brown, put 1kg of haricot beans and a couple of large *botifarra*—you can also use *botifarra negre*, or blood sausage, for this—into the casserole, along with one glass of white wine, a spray of mint, a bay leaf and another 250g of bacon. Season with salt, black pepper and sugar and let it cook until the beans are tender. Add one *barreja* (or a shot glass) of mixed anisette and muscatel,

Kitten Fleming

before serving. An alternative version: fry 1 kg of sausages in olive oil until golden, then remove them from the pan. Into the oil put 2 tablespoons of flour or breadcrumbs, a teaspoon of tomato puree, a glass of white wine and a glass of stock. Stir and cook for 10 minutes before sieving. Blanch 24 peeled cloves of garlic. Return the sausages to the pan, adding the garlic, a bouquet garni and a piece of dried orange peel. Pour the sieved sauce over the sausages and cook gently for half an hour. The result will be delicious and perfectly complemented by a glass of full-bodied Catalonian red wine.

...and wining

In recent years, Catalonian wine producers have begun to receive international recognition for their innovative approach to winemaking. The most famous are from the Penedès region. After forming a partnership with the Jean León winery, Miguel Torres introduced cabernet and chardonnay grapes into his *bodegas*, thereby bringing the consistency and strength of New World-style production to Catalonia. Try his superb Mas la Plana Cabernet or Milmanda Chardonnay for world quality wines. Penedès, of course, is renowned for its Cava, made from a blend of three local grapes, Parellada, Macabeo and Xarello. This lean, dry sparkling wine, usually drunk as an aperitif, was first produced in the late 19th-century by Manuel Raventós at his Codorníu estate after he'd worked in the Champagne region of France. Compare with Codorníu's Cavas with up-and-coming Juvé y Camps or Segura Viudas and decide for yourself which is better on the palate. The Penedès region is now challenged for supremacy by other *denominació d'origen* areas such as Empordà, Monsant and particularly Priorat. The cold nights and hot days of the mountainous Priorat region near Tarragona are responsible for intense, blockbuster reds from the Scala Dei and Rocafort de Queralt *bodegas*.

Commons.wikimedia.org / Emi Yañez / Andrew Fogg

cityNights

From opera on La Rambla to rave in the Raval, Barcelona's entertainment scene covers all tastes and types. The best way to find out what's on is to consult the weekly *Guía del Ocio* (Spanish) or *Time Out* (Catalan) or the English-language listings magazine *Barcelona Metropolitan*, which can be picked up at bars and hotels. You'll also find a useful local arts and events section in the Barcelona-based *La Vanguardia* and the national daily *El País*. The tourist offices also have information on major concerts and events, and the branch in Plaça Catalunya has a ticket office.

Barcelona is a late-night city—its clubs don't get going before 1am; and some are still in full party mode at 5 or 6am. Drinks are pricey but measures are a lot larger than in other European cities. Dress should be smart-casual and you may often have to queue to get in. Note that nightlife noise has become a big issue in Barcelona, and rowdy revellers on the street are frequently frowned upon.

◄ *Barcelona is well known for its exuberant party scene.*

MAJOR ARTS VENUES

Gran Teatre del Liceu
✧ Liceu
La Rambla 51–59
☎ 93 485 99 00
Open daily. Guided tours at 10am.
Barcelona's grand 19th-century opera house burnt down in 1994 but was rebuilt and transformed into a cutting-edge, high-tech venue, with the auditorium still in the original style. El Liceu's programme has diversified from classic opera to ballet and even flamenco.

L'Auditori
✧ Marina, Monumental
C/de Lepant 150
☎ 93 247 93 00
Home to the Barcelona Symphony Orchestra and Catalunya National Orchestra, this huge new theatre house is blessed with superb acoustics. The concerts often combine mainstream classical music with works by modern Catalan composers and even jazz.

Mercat de les Flors
✧ Espanya, Poble Sec
C/Lleida 59
☎ 93 256 26 00
Former flower market turned into a three-hall venue for music, dance and theatre, including English-language productions. It's the centrepiece of the new Ciutat del Teatre, which also incorporates the spectacular new showcase home of the Institut del Teatre, Catalunya's performing arts academy and theatrical body.

Palau de la Música Catalana
✧ Urquinaona
C/Palau de la Música 4-6
Guided tours daily 10am–3.30pm, to 6pm Easter week and July, to 8pm in August. Advance purchase recommended; available from Palau de la Música Ticket Office or their website (www.palaumusica.cat)
☎ 90 247 54 85
Domènech i Montaner's magnificent Modernista theatre provides an unforgettable setting for orchestral classical music and performances of choral music by the Orfeó Catalá choir.

Sala Apolo and La [2] de Apolo
✧ Paral.lel
C/Nou de la Rambla 111–113
☎ 93 441 40 01
The management of this old music hall has an acute nose for new talent in rock, pop and all its subgenres. After gigs have ended Sala Apolo turns into a nightclub. Next door a newer, smaller theatre (called La [2]) hosts flamenco, cabaret and karaoke.

Sala Razzmatazz
✧ La Bogatell
C/Almogàvers 122
☎ 93 320 82 00
Major national and international pop and rock artists, or at least those who can't fill a stadium, generally end up in this venue in the depths of Poblenou, away from noise-sensitive neighbours. Post concert, the place turns into a packed out nightclub.

Teatre Nacional de Catalunya
✧ Glòries, Monumental
Plaça de les Arts 1
☎ 93 306 57 07
Guided tours Tues and Thurs 10am–1pm
☎ 93 306 57 49
Vast theatre putting on drama and dance productions from Catalonia, Spain and the rest of Europe.

BARS AND LIVE MUSIC

Antilla BCN Latin Club
✥ Hospital Clínic, Urgell
C/Aragó 141
☎ 65 224 73 48
Closed Mon and Tues
Salsa to the strains of Latin and Caribbean bands. If you can't dance, their in-house teachers will show you how.

Bar Marsella
✥ Liceu
C/Sant Pau 65
☎ 93 442 72 63
This century old bar is famous for serving *absenta*, the supposedly hallucogenic tipple favoured by Jean Genet and other bohemians who trod the Barri Xino. Despite being frequented by tourists, its dusty decadence has remained intact.

Bikini
✥ Les Corts, Maria Cristina
Avda Diagonal 547
☎ 93 322 08 00
Nightclub open Wed–Sat. Concerts vary at other times.
Check website (www.bikinibcn.com)
Eclectic artists ranging from Latin American to, rap, reggae and swing

and post-concert nightclub.

Dry Martini
✥ Diagonal
C/Aribau 162–166
☎ 93 217 50 72
This classic cocktail bar is a city institution. Take a seat at the mahogany bar or one of the plush velvet settees and let the white-coated waiters guide you through the most extensive drinks list in town.

El Tablao de Carmen
✥ Espanya
Poble Espanyol,
C/Francesc Ferrer i Guàrdia 13
☎ 93 325 68 95
Closed Mon. Flamenco show at 7pm and 9.30pm
A traditional flamenco *tablao* with live music and dancing. Booking essential (www.tablaodecarmen.com). Dinner and tapas options available.

Ginger
✥ Jaume I
C/Palma de Sant Just 1
☎ 93 310 53 09
Closed Sun and Mon
Sophisticated *tapas* and a wide selection of wines and *cavas*. Relaxed atmosphere, with classic surroundings.

Harlem Jazz Club
✥ Jaume I
C/Comtessa de Sobradiel 8
☎ 93 310 07 55
Closed Sun and Mon
Jazz, Rock, Latin and African rythms in the heart of the medieval old town. Gigs start at 10pm.

Heliogàbal
✥ Joanic
C/Ramón y Cajal 80
Concerts start around 10pm
Solo artists and acoustic groups, mainly of the folk, country and experimental ilk, perform in the back room of this popular bar, a meeting point for hip locals in the Gràcia area.

Jamboree
✥ Liceu
Plaça Reial 17
☎ 93 319 17 89
Most concerts start at 8pm
Perennially popular jazz, funk and blues venue, with a late-night club after the bands have finished.

JazzSí Club
✥ Sant Antoni
C/Requesens 2
☎ 93 329 00 20
Most gigs start around 8.30pm
Next to the music school, this small bar has gigs

most nights, from blues to jazz to flamenco. The entry price includes a drink.

La Vinya del Senyor
✦ Jaume I
Plaça Santa Maria 5
☎ 93 310 33 79
Facing the beautiful façade of the Santa Maria del Mar church, this small wine bar has an enviable position. It is tight for space inside, and the outside tables are always sought after. The wine list is extensive and the view memorable.

Luz de Gas
✦ Diagonal
C/Muntaner 246
☎ 93 209 77 11
In a delightful old theatre, join the crowd to hear soul music, funk, blues, trad and modern jazz.

Marula Cafè
✦ Drassanes, Liceu
C/Escudillers 49
Closed on Mon and Tue
Lively bar-club that celebrates "black" music in all its glory, from funk to soul, reggae to rap. Occasional live gigs and jam sessions.

Milano
✦ Catalunya, Universitat
Ronda Universitat 35
☎ 93 112 71 50

Amongst the nocturnal no man's land of Plaça Catalunya, this basement bar-club is a beacon of light, with a sophisticated atmosphere, great cocktails and live jazz ensembles late in the week.

Negroni
✦ Universitat
C/Joaquín Costa 46
☎ 61 942 92 71
On a street packed with bars this tiny venue stands out for its quality cocktails and trendy-yet-comfortable decor.

Schilling
✦ Liceu, Jaume I
C/Ferrán 23
☎ 93 317 67 87
One of the city's main points for pre-nightclub drinking, this bar/café is packed day and night.

Tinta Roja
✦ Poble Sec
C/Creu dels Molers 17
☎ 93 443 32 43
Closed Sun–Tues
Furnished with mix matched sofas and armchairs, velvet curtains and sparkly chandeliers, this tango club transports you back to old Buenos Aires. Tango classes on Wed at 8.30pm–10pm and anything from folk, to art performances on other days.

NIGHTCLUBS

Cabaret Berlin
✦ Tetuan, Universitat
C/Bailén 22
☎ 93 481 51 91
Thurs–Sat only
Barcelona's hipsters flock to this intimate club that, as the name suggests, has an ambiance of underground Berlin. Guest Dj's and nightly performances of the burlesque nature create a decadent vibe.

Café Royale
✦ Liceu, Drassanes
C/Nou de Zurbano 3
☎ 93 318 89 56
Closed Sun and Mon
Just off the Plaça Reial, this intimate, cosmopolitan dance club plays classic soul, jazz and Latin tunes to a slightly older crowd. The sophisticated decor is reminiscent of a classic cocktail bar.

CDLC – Carpe Diem Lounge Club
✦ Ciutadella–Vila Olímpica
Passeig Marítim 32
☎ 93 224 04 70
Cool club on the beach where beautiful people open their wallets. The terrace is the best place to shoot the evening breeze.

City Hall
✦ Catalunya
Rambla de
Catalunya 2–4
☎ 93 233 33 33
Opens every night from 11pm
Popular central night club that spins different music each night, from rap to house, to an ecstatic crowd. Small outside terrace to cool down.

Club Catwalk
✦ Ciutadella–Vila Olímpica
C/Ramón Fargas
☎ 93 221 61 61
Open Thurs–Sun
Club Catwalk is one of the less pretentious nightclubs in the Vila Olímpica, where the focus is on good, quality dance music as opposed to fashion statements.

Eclipse
Bus 64
Hotel W,
Plaça Rosa dels Vents 1
☎ 93 295 28 00
Up on the 26th floor and overlooking the sea, the Eclipse club of the W Hotel is the latest city hot spot. Dress up and get down to London Djs or get there early evening for a cocktail and sushi.

Elephant
✦ Palau Reial
Pg. dels Til.lers 1
☎ 93 334 02 58
Thurs–Sat only
This uptown, see-and-be-seen club attracts the beautiful people to its faux-Arabic lounge and dance floor.

Moog
✦ Liceu, Drassanes
C/de l'Arc del Teatre 3
☎ 93 319 17 89
Daily from midnight
One of the city's evergreen clubs: upstairs is a 1970s retro disco, and down below, a power-house techno dancefloor.

Otto Zutz
🚇 Gràcia
C/de Lincoln 15
☎ 93 238 07 22
Closed Sun–Tues
Its three floors fill up with Barcelona's sleekest clubbers—lots of students, and VIPs on the top floor.

BOOKING YOUR SEAT

Tickets can be purchased by going directly to the theatre, but most people use one of the various on-line ticketing services such as **Telentrada** (www.telentrada.com) or **Ticketmaster** (www.ticketmaster.es). Telentrada is run the the local bank Catalunya Caixa, and after choosing your seat on-line and paying with your credit card, tickets are picked up either at the venue before the performance or through one of Catalunya Caixa's auto-matic tellers. If you purchase your tickets through Ticketmaster, you can pick them up via a ServiCaixa vending machine. **FNAC**, a large music and entertainment store in Plaça Catalunya also has a ticket office on the ground floor. Many nightclubs have their own on-line booking platforms; this saves you from having to queue in the street, which can take be time-consuming.

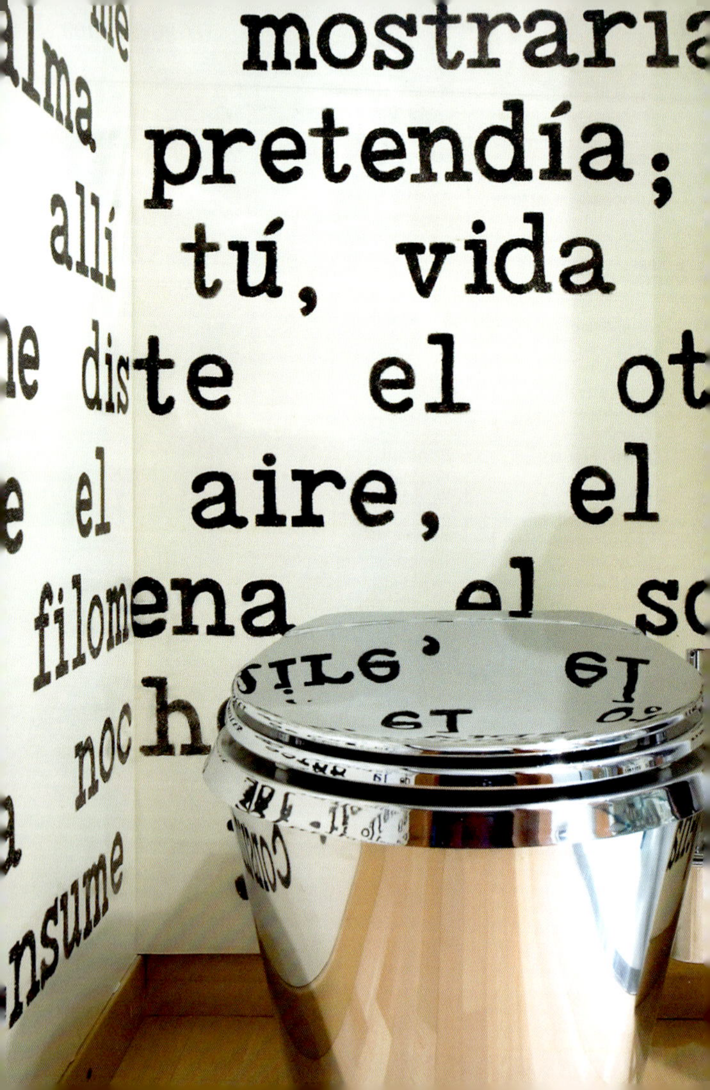

alma mostraria
pretendía;
allí tú, vida
e diste el ot
e el aire, el
filomena el so
noc h
nsume

cityFacts

istockphoto.com/herrero de Frutos

◀ *Even toilets in Barcelona are aesthetically designed to astonish visitors!*

Airports

Barcelona's El Prat airport lies 12 km (7.5 miles) southwest of the city and consists of two terminals (T1 and T2). Both are serviced by the Aerobus, which leaves every ten minutes from 5.30am to 00.30am for Plaça de Catalunya in central Barcelona and takes about 35 minutes. There's also a cheaper (yet slightly longer) train service that leaves from T2 to Barcelona-Sants station, departing every half hour. If you arrive at T1, you can take the free shuttle bus that connects the two terminals to the station (think twice about doing it in a taxi, as drivers are currently charging 20 euros for the five-minute journey). On your outward journey, make sure you know which terminal you are leaving from, as there is a separate Aerobus for each one. Taxis from both cost about 25–30 euros to central Barcelona. There is a €4.20 airport surcharge. Taxi ranks can be found immediately outside the terminals. ☎ 90 240 47 04 for general airport information, or www.aena.es.

The vast majority of airlines use the newer, and much sleeker T1. Some low-cost airlines (including Ryanair) arrive at T2, which has the advantage of being connected to the train station. However, you'll find tourist information booths, car hire and money exchange at both. T1 has the advantage of plenty of shops and restaurants—you may want to arrive a little early on your way out!

Bicycle Hire

Barcelona is very cycle-friendly as evident by the plentiful bike lanes and Bicing, the red and white bikes you see swooshing all over the city. Unfortunately these are only available to residents (or those that are prepared to wait the ten days for the membership card to arrive, see: www.bicing.com) but bike rental services abound, particularly in the Ciutat Vella. Among them, Bike Rental Barcelona has folding and ergo bikes and will deliver to your hotel. ☎ 66 605 76 55. You can take a tour of the city with Barcelona CicloTour ☎ 93 317 19 70, C/Tallers 45. Tours leave from outside the Hard Rock Café on Plaça Catalunya at 11am, 4.30pm and 7.30pm (Fri, Sat, Sun, in summer only) and no reservation is necessary—just turn up 10 minutes before departure time. For those who want to take it easy, Rent Electric can supply you with battery-operated bikes, scooters and tuk-tuks ☎ 67 047 44 74, www.rentelectric.com.

The majority of bikes lanes can be found in the Ciutat Vella, the Eixample and along the beaches, and it's legal to cycle on a footpath over three meters wide. Wearing a helmet is compulsory for children under 16, and rental services should provide you with one, as well as child's seat. If you plan to stop off along the way, don't forget to ask for a lock, as bike theft is common. Barcelona traffic is becoming more and more bike aware, but do take precautions when turning corners, obey the bike "traffic lights" and use hand signals.

Climate

The city enjoys a fine, Mediterranean climate. Late spring, early summer and autumn can be marvellously warm and fresh, though there's always the chance of seasonal downpours. July and August are usually very hot and humid, with temperatures reaching up to 37°C—you'll probably find yourself searching for a spot that catches a sea breeze. Winters are often clear and bright, though can be very cold, a reminder of Barcelona's proximity to the Pyrenees.

For detailed weather predictions for Catalunya: www.meteo.cat.

Customs

EU regulations apply. Visitors aged 17 years or older, travelling from a country outside the EU can import, duty-free, 200 cigarettes, one litre of spirits over 22° or 2 litres spirits or aperitifs less than 22°, and 4 litres wine and 16 litres beer. For passengers travelling from other EU countries, there is no limit on the quantity of purchases imported for personal consumption if they are duty-paid.

Disabled Visitors

With many narrow, uneven sidewalks and historic buildings, general mobility for disabled travellers isn't particularly easy in Barcelona, but things are improving all the time. Some ramps for wheelchairs are installed along the beaches in summer, allowing access to the water. New public buldings—and renovations to old ones—have been constucted with the needs of the mobility-challenged in mind. The city's buses, the airport bus, the tram network and many of its taxis are also equipped to take passengers in wheelchairs. Lines 2 and 11 of the metro system have been constructed with wheel-chair friendly access, whilst most older ones have lifts installed at one of the exits. You can check which stations have been adapted on the website www.tmb.net. Some Bus Turistic vehicles have ramps, as do all the trams. For information on facilities at a given museum or restaurant, call direct or contact ECOM, an umbrella association of disabled organizations, ☎ 93 451 55 50. British expatriate Craig Grimes talks about visiting Barcelona, as well as many other cities, in a wheelchair on his website: www.craiggrimes.com.

Driving

If you decide to take a car into the centre, it's probably a good idea to use a car park rather than risk leaving it on the street, where resident-only parking is now the norm. Large car parks can be found in the centre at Plaça dels Ángels, near the MACBA gallery, and Moll de la Fusta, by the port; Plaça de Catalunya, Plaça Seu (Cathedral) and Plaça Urquinaona—look out for the blue interactive signs that point to the nearest car park and place availability. Alternatively, you can use one of the BSM car parks, which are run by the local council. If you buy a pre-paid tarjeta, the hourly rate works out at just under 2 euros for 100 hours and can be used at any of the 50 car parks in their network. BSM also have a special car parks adapted for caravans and mobile homes. For more information see: www.aparcamentsbsm.cat.

A car is useful if you plan to do a lot of touring beyond Barcelona. Note that the speed limit in town is 40 kph (25 mph), while on other roads it varies between 80 kph (50 mph) and 120 kph (75 mph); watch out for the signs! Those caught speeding will face on-the-spot fines. If you bring your own car, be sure to carry your driving license, car registration document, valid insurance certificate (check that your insurance covers driving in Spain before you leave) and two warning triangles and a yellow safety vest in case of a breakdown. Catalonia's main automobile club is the Reial Automòbil Club de Catalunya (RACC). Ask at your own automobile club before you leave whether it is affiliated to the RACC. ☎ 90 215 61 56 for 24-hour breakdown assistance; ☎ 90 245 24 52 for information.

A simpler option might be to hire a car when you are in Barcelona. All the big car hire firms have offices at the airport and in town. It's worth shopping around as well as trying local firms often have good deals on offer. Try Pepe Car, ☎ 80 741 42 43, www.pepecar.com or Sixt, ☎ 90 249 16 16, www.sixt.es. You will need to show a valid driving license, be over 21 (in most cases), and have a credit card for the deposit.

Emergencies

Ambulance: ☎ 112; Fire brigade: ☎ 112; Police: ☎ 112

The Turisme-Atenció police station of the Guàrdia Urbana (City Police) at La Rambla 43, ☎ 092 (the general number for police enquires), is designed for tourists who need to report a crime. Officers speak English and French, though you will be more than likely directed to the *comisaría* of the Mossos d'Esquadra (Catalan Police) around the corner at Nou de la Rambla 43 if you want to file an official report (*denúncia*). Both stations are open 24 hours a day. You can also file a *denúncia* via the internet on the website www.policiadecatalunya.net, though you will still need to take it to a police station to be verified.

For urgent medical attention head for a hospital casualty department *(Urgències)*. The following are centrally located:

Centre d'Urgències, Peracamps, Av. Drassanes 13–15, ☎ 93 441 06 00

Hospital Clínic, C/Villarroel 170, ☎ 93 227 54 00

For dental emergencies:

Clinica Dental, C/Pau Claris, 194–196, ☎ 93 487 83 29 (Daily 9am-midnight)

Permanent 24-hour pharmacies include:

Farmàcia Clapés, La Rambla 98, ☎ 93 301 28 43

Farmàcia Cervera, C/Muntaner 254, ☎ 93 200 09 96

Entry Formalities

Most visitors only require a valid passport to enter the country. No visa is needed for North American, Australian and New Zealand citizens for stays of up to 3 months.

Health

EU nationals are entitled to free medical care in a case of emergency, as long as they hold a European Health Card. Non-EU citizens should ascertain whether their country has reciprocal arrangements with Spain. If not, it would be wise to take out health insurance before the journey.

Language
In addition to Catalan, most Barceloneses speak Spanish (*castellano*—Castilian—as it is known there). Catalan is not a dialect of Spanish, rather it's a separate Romance language derived from Latin and with close affinities to Provençal, a language of southern France. At larger hotels, shops and restaurants staff will probably speak some English.

Lost and Found
If you lose something on public transport you can check for it the following day at the TMB information office at Diagonal Metro Station. If you have lost something around town (or have it stolen), contact the city's lost-and-found office. This is where items handed into police stations end up:

Troballes de Ajuntament de Barcelona
Plaça Pi i Sunyer 10, ☎ 010 or 93 413 20 31
For items lost in taxis, try the Institut Metropolità del Taxi, ☎ 93 223 51 51.
For anything lost at the airport, call the main information desk:
☎ 90 240 47 04.

Money Matters
Currency. The Euro, divided into 100 cents. Coins: 1, 2, 5, 10, 20 and 50 cents, 1 and 2 euros; banknotes: 5, 10, 20, 50, 100, 200 and 500 euros.
Banks. Generally open Mon–Fri 8.30am–2pm. La Caixa bank has branches at Barcelona's airport in T1 (daily 7.30am-10.00pm) and T2 (daily 7.30am-8.30pm). Both terminals have cash machines. Exchange bureaux (*cambio* or *canvi*) can be found around town and stay open late, but the rates tend not to be as good as those of banks.
Cash Cards. You can draw cash with your card if it carries the Visa or MasterCard symbol, at most ATM cash machines using your regular PIN code number. Keep in mind that many ATMs in the old city now close after 11pm.
Credit Cards. They are widely accepted in hotels, restaurants and shops. You have to show some form of photo ID when making a retail purchase with a credit card, even if it requires a pin.

Post Office

In general they open Mon–Fri 8.30am–8.30pm (some close at 2.30pm), Sat 9.30am–1pm. The main post office at Plaça d'Antonio López near Port Vell keeps longer hours, opening Mon–Fri 8.30am–9.30pm, Sat 8.30am–2pm for sale of stamps, stationery, and with fax and poste restante facilities as well. Stamps can also be bought at most *estancos* (tobacconists).

Public Holidays

Be prepared to find Barcelona's banks, shops and many of its restaurants, galleries and museums closed on the following public holidays:

Jan 1	New Year's Day
Jan 6	Epiphany
May 1	May Day
June 24	St John the Baptist
Aug 15	Assumption
Sept 11	Catalan National Day
Sept 24	Our Lady of Mercy
Oct 12	Spanish National Day
Nov 1	All Saints' Day
Dec 6	Constitution Day
Dec 8	Immaculate Conception
Dec 25	Christmas Day
Dec 26	Boxing Day

Movable:
March/April Good Friday (*Divendres Sant*), Easter Monday (*Pasqua Florida*)
May/June Whit Monday (*Pasqua Granada*)

Public Transport

Barcelona has a first-rate public transport network of ⬛ FGC trains, ⬛ RENFE state trains, ◆ metro trains and trams, the latter three being run by the city transport authority (TMB). Metro lines operate to midnight, extend their service to 2am on Fridays and run 24 hrs on Saturdays. FGC operate from about 5am to midnight. Buses run from around 6am to 10pm with a night service on several routes, picked up from Plaça de Catalunya.

Information:

TMB   ☎ 90 207 50 27, www.tmb.cat

FGC   ☎ 93 012 15 15, www.fgc.cat

RENFE ☎ 90 232 03 20

Note that if you intend to take a long distance train, it's advisable to book in advance.

There's the same flat fare for a single journey on metro, FGC trains and bus, € 2.15. There is a variety of options for multi-trip tickets for central Barcelona, all giving significant reductions. The Tarjeta T-10 is a carnet of ten tickets costing € 10.30, valid on metro, FGC trains, inner-city RENFE trains, trams and buses; it can be shared by two or more people. The Tarjeta T-Mes costs € 52.75 and allows unlimited trips within 30 days accross the network, but cannot be shared.

And then there are the travelcards, Hola BCN!, well worth the investment if you do a lot of travelling around. The cards entitle you to unlimited transport on the metro underground, buses and trams in Barcelona city centre. You also receive discounts on entry tickets to many of Barcelona's main attractions. The Hola BCN! 2 Dies gives two days of travel for € 14, the 3 Dies three days for € 20 the 4 Dies is € 25.50 and the 5 Dies € 30.50.

The double-decker Barcelona Bus Turístic is a convenient way for tourists to discover the most interesting sights. You can hop on and off as many times as you like at any of the stops. The three different tourist tours can be combined on the same ticket (change at six transfer stops). Audioguides are provided, and the buses run every 5 to 25 minutes depending on season. Tickets can be bought on the bus, at the Turisme de Barcelona information centres, TMB customer service centres and online at www.tmb.cat. 1-day adult € 27, children 4–12 € 16; 2-day adult (consecutive) € 38, children € 20. Vouchers for discounts are given with the tickets.

Safety

Barcelona is a fairly safe city for travellers, although petty crime such as pickpocketing and bag-snatching in the crowded tourist areas such as La Rambla and the Barri Gòtic is frequent. It's always sensible to carry out a few basic safety measures. Only carry the money you will need for the day along with a credit card and ATM card.

Be careful where you place valuables, wallets, cameras etc and keep a firm grip on handbags and shoulder bags in crowded places, cafés and restaurants. If possible, leave airline tickets, traveller's cheques and extra cash in your hotel safe.

Taxis

The city's black-and-yellow taxis are a reasonable option, especially for two or three people travelling together. They cost more outside normal working hours and a supplement will be added for trips to and from the airport, from Sants train station and the ferry terminal and after 8pm on Public Holidays. Many cabs accept credit card payment.

Taxi ranks can be found throughout Barcelona at most of the big squares and railway stations, and taxis can also be hailed in the street if they have their green roof-light on. They should also have a sign in the windscreen saying *lliure/libre*, "free".

Reputable firms include:

Barna Taxi ☎ 93 322 22 22
Radio Taxi ☎ 93 293 31 11

Telephone and Internet

The international code for Spain is 34; Barcelona numbers all start with 93. To make an international call dial 00, the country code (US and Canada 1, UK 44), area code and local number. You can make overseas calls from public pay phones, or one of the many *locutorios* (call centres) dotted around the old city. These also sell cut-rate phonecards, which can be used from any fixed or mobile phone for local or international calls. *Locutorio* options are much cheaper than using either hotel room phones or roaming rates. There are plenty of "hot spots" in bars, cafés and many hotels supply this service free of charge. You can also tap into the free 'Barcelona WiFi' service at public libraries, museums, civic centers, enclosed parks etc.—just search for the signal. Most *locutorios* also offer internet.

Time

From the last Sunday in March to the last Sunday in October, Barcelona follows GMT +2. In winter, it becomes GMT +1.

Tipping

Service is never included in restaurant bills (the 10% charge you see on the check is sales tax), so you will need to leave a tip, normally 5–10%. It's also customary to give a 5% tip to taxi drivers, leave the small change in bars and cafés, and tip a small amount to hotel porters and toilet attendants.

Toilets

You won't find public toilets in plentiful supply in Barcelona. Luckily, bar and café owners are usually pretty relaxed about letting you use the facilities if you make a purchase at the bar. Alternatively, make sure you take advantage of the toilets in museums, galleries and restaurants while you're there, as these are often the most spick and span. In summer, there are plenty of public toilets along the city's beaches and a discreetly nipping to the ground floor toilets in the large hotels is also a good option.

Tourist Information Offices

The main tourist office of the Turisme de Barcelona is situated beneath Plaça de Catalunya, open daily 9.30am–9.30pm; ☎ 93 285 38 34 (Mon–Fri 8am–8pm). It's good for maps, city information and souvenirs and does foreign exchange, tax refund and theatre and performance tickets. There are also branches at the Barcelona-Sants railway station, the airport (both T1 and T2), next to the City Hall in Plaça Sant Jaume, the cruise ship terminal and information booths outside some of the main attractions, with restricted opening hours.

The Catalan government also runs offices providing tourist information on the region. Head office:

Palau Robert, Passeig de Gràcia 107, ☎ 93 238 80 91
Mon–Sat 10am–8pm; Sun 10am–2.30pm
They also have offices at the airport in both Terminal A and Terminal B.

For up-to-date information on sites in Barcelona, call the City Hall Information Service, ☎ 010. For the rest of Catalunya: ☎ 012.

Voltage

Electric current is 220-volt 50-cycle AC, and sockets are for plugs with two round pins. British and American equipment will require an adaptor.

Parc Güell

1 300 m

N

Hospital
Militar

Carrer de Josep
Jover

Centre
Mèdic
Delfos

Carrer d'Esteve Terradas

Avinguda de L'Hospital Militar

Carrer del Baró de la Barre

Passatge

C. de Montomés

Cardedeu

C. de Castellterçol

Marianel

Pl. de
Tona

Parc
la Creueta del Coll

Coll

del

Carrer

C. Font del Coll

C. de Santuari

Bda. Beat

Almató

C. d'Ebre

C. Mora
la Mora

Av. Santa Maria

Bda.
Solanell

Móra

C. Duran
i Borell

Plaça
Gibraltar

de Gustavo Bécquer

Carrer del

C. de les Balears

Ptge. de Tona

Pl. de
Flandes

Mare

Carrer

de

Carrer

Rubens

del Remei

del Torrent

Plata de
Montserrat

Font del Remei

C. de Tirso

C. del
Portell

Avinguda de

Passeig

Carrer de Sant

Eudald

C. de Pere

C. del Riu de la Plata

Cami de Ca

Carrer
de Ceuta

C. de les
Coves d'en
Cimany

Pl. de
Mons

Fargola

Sant Camil

Viaducte Vallcarca

Avinguda de la República

Vallcarca

Vallcarca

Bda.
Blanes

C. La
Argentera

Carrer de la

Ptge

de Coll

Monte carmel

Casa Trias

Ptge la
Costa

Turull

de Agramunt

les Medes Baixada de Briz

Parc Güell

**Plaça de la Natura
i sala Hipòstila**

**Casa-museu
Gaudí**

Avinguda

Ptge
d'Espíria

Verdi

de

Baixada de Vallcarca

Baixada

de la

Repartidor

Sostres

Glòria

Avinguda del

Carrer de Can Mora

Carretera
del Carmel

C. de
Ballester

C. de
Velázquez

C. de
Bolívar

de
Mare

Carrer

Carrer

del

Carrer

Carrer

dels Albígesos

Turó de
les tres creus

del Portel

Escalinata i el drac

Carrer d'Olot

**Pavellons
de l'entrada**

C. de Marianao

C. de Josep Cottolengo

Pau negre

Ptge
Napoleó

C. de Valldoreix

Carrer de Sant

Rbla.
de Mercedes

C. de
Mercedes

Sta
Eleonor

C. d'Antequera

C. de
Mollet

Avinguda de Pompeu Fabra

Saujalat

Carrer de Maignon

**Reial Santuari
Sant Josep de
la Muntanya**

Avinguda de Sant Josep de la Muntanya

Ptge
Mercedes

C. de Pare Jacint Alegre

Cugat
del Vallès

C. de la
Mare

C. de
Miquel

C. de Can Toda

i Badia

Pl. de
Lesseps

Lesseps

**Mercat de
Lesseps**

Muntanya

Carrer de
Sta Perpètua

Ptge de
Frígola

Travessera de Dalt

**Hospital
de l'Esperança**

Travessera de Dalt

C. de
Miquel

de la Salut

Av. de la Mare de
Déu de Montserrat

Secretari Coloma

Gràcia

C. Pérez Galdós

C. de
Nil
Fabra

C. de
Betlem

C. de
Santa
Àgata

C. de
Topazi

C. Maurici
Serrahima

C. Bellver

Verdi

Carrer de Torrent

Ventallat

Carrer

Pl. del
Nord

Pl. del

C. d'Alzina

Carrer del

C. de Vilafranca

C. de Martí

Massens

Sant

Carrer de les Flors

Carrer del Torrent de les Flors

Cardener

C. de Martí

Rabassa

San Miguel
de los Santos

Salvador

**Hospital
Evangèlic**

Carrer de l'Escorial

Carrer de les Camèlies

Trav. Vella de Dalt

Balcells

C. de Pg. d'Amunt

**Clínica Ntra Sra
del Remei**

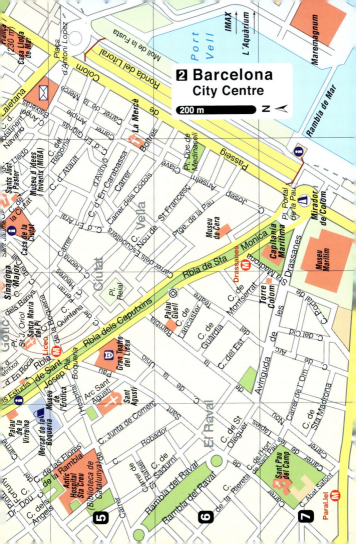

Around Barcelona

3 ⬛ 300 m ➤ N

Parc natural
Montnegre-
Corredor

Caldes
d'Estrac
Port del
Balis
Canyamars
St Vicenç
de Montalt
St Andreu
de Llavaneres
Dosrius
Mataró
Sta Agnès
La Roca
del Vallès
Argentona
Cabrera
de Mar
Vilassar de Mar
Premià de Mar
Granollers
Canovelles
Vilanova
del Vallès
Montmelo 534 m Orrius
Cabrils Vilassar
de Dalt
El Masnou
el Tenes
Llíçà
d'Amunt
Parets
Montornès
del Vallès
Vallromanas
Premià
de Dalt
Alella Teià
Montgat
Lliçà
de Vall
Mollet
del Vallès
Martorelles
Tiana
Caldes de
Montbui
Sentmenat
Palau de
Plegamans
la Salut
Sta Perpètua
Montcada
i Reixac
St Adrià
de Besòs
Badalona
Sagrada
Família
Castellar
del Vallès
St Julià
St Feliu
del Racó
Torre-
bonica
La Salut
Polinyà
del Vallès
Barberà
La
Llagosta
Ripollet
B-20
Monestir
de Pedralbes
Barcelona
Montjuic
El Prat
de Llobregat
Sabadell
Barberà
del Vallès
Cerdanyola
Monestir
de St Cugat
Sant Cugat
del Vallès
La Floresta
Tibidabo
Valldoreix
L'Hospitalet
St Quirze
St Llorenç
del Munt
La Mola
Matadepera
Ullastrell
El Papiol
St Just
Desvern
St Feliu
St Boi
de Llobregat
Sant
de Llobregat
Aéroport del
Prat Barcelona
1095 m
Parc natural
de Sant Llorenç
del Munt
Terrassa
Rubí
Castellbisbal
Vallirana
Els Molins
de Rei
Colònia
Güell
Viladecans
Gavà
Viladecavalls
Ullastrell
El Palau
St Andreu
de la Barca
Corbera
de Dalt
Sant Vicenç
dels Horts
Sta Coloma
de Cervelló
Begues
Castell
d'Eramprunya
Martorell
Pallejà
St Climent
de Ll.
Sant Cova
Olesa de
Montserrat
el Llobregat
Castellví
de Rosanes
Corbera
de Ll.
La Palma
Torrelles de Ll.
Relinars
Castellbell
Esparreguera
Abrera
Can Amat
St Esteve
Sesrovires
St Llorenç
d'Hortons
Col de la
Creu d'Ordal
Olesa de
Bonesvalls
Monistrol
de M.
Montserrat
Monestir
Sta Cova
Collbató
Gelida
Ordal
Parc natural
de Garraf
Olivella
La Morella ▲ 595 m

Costa Daurada

Editors:
Petronella Greenhalgh
Eleonora Di Campli

Research:
Suzanne Wales

Layout:
Matias Jolliet
Luc Malherbe

Maps:
JPM Publications S.A.

Copyright © 2015, 2009
by JPM Publications S.A.
12, avenue William-Fraisse
1006 Lausanne
Suisse
information@jpmguides.com
http://www.jpmguides.com/

Every care has been taken
to verify the information in
the guide, but neither the
publisher nor his client can
accept responsibility for any
errors that may have occur-
red. If you spot an inaccuracy
or a serious omission, please
let us know.

Printed in Germany
13289.00.14457
Edition 2015